THE
EVERYTHING®

WEDDING
SHOWER
BOOK

Thrill the bride and amaze the guests with a celebration to remember

Je...

Adams Media Corporation
Holbrook, Massachusetts

An Everything® Series Book.
Everything® is a registered trademark
of Adams Media Corporation.

Published by Adams Media Corporation
260 Center Street, Holbrook, MA 02343

ISBN: 1-58062-188-0

Printed in Canada.

J I H G F E D C B

Library of Congress Cataloging-in-Publication Data
Jenkins, Jennifer.
The everything wedding shower book / by Jennifer Jenkins.
      p.   cm.
         ISBN 1-58062-188-0
  1. Showers (Parties) 2. Weddings. I. Title.
         GV1472.7.S5J46   2000
         793.2—dc21   99-048060

Many of the designations used by manufactures and sellers to dis-
tinguish their products are claimed as trademarks. Where those designations have appear in this book and Adams Media was aware
of a trademark claim, the designations have been printed in initial
capital letters.

Illustrations by Barry Littmann and Kathie Kelleher.

*This book is available at quantity discounts for bulk purchases.
For information, call 1-800-872-5627.*

Visit our home page at http://www.adamsmedia.com

Contents

Chapter 2
Shower Themes 23

Chapter 3
Show Me the Money!
How to Budget the Shower 59

Chapter 4
Choosing a Venue 67

Chapter 5
Inviting the Guests 73

Chapter 6
Ringing the Dinner Bell..........................87

Chapter 7
Decorating Your Party:
All about Room Decorations..............107

Chapter 8
Women Bearing Gifts 133

Chapter 9
Seamless Party Management..............141

Chapter 10
Cha-Cha-Cha-Choices:
Getting the Right Music

Chapter 11
Great Shower Activities, or How
to Entertain a Bunch of Women
for Two Hours

Chapter 12
Parting Gifts..173

Chapter 13
Cleanup Tricks 181

Index 185

Introduction

S o she's getting married! And *you* are the dear friend who wants to throw her the perfect shower. You want a shower that is a tribute to the friendship you share, a shower that she—and all the other guests—will remember forever, with fond memories.

This nifty little book will show you how. It's got the right title—it will tell you **Everything** you need to know. Using the clever tricks and tips you will find here, you will be able to throw her a terrific shower. It will be one that suits your budget, your personality, and your schedule just about perfectly.

The goal of reading this book is for you to get the skills to throw the most wonderful shower with the minimum of expense and fuss. You'll find all sorts of great ideas, tips, secrets, helpful hints, and planning tools to help you pull it all off. Sound too good to be true? It's not. The things you will learn here will make this an occasion to remember—and perhaps rival the *fun quotient* of the wedding she's working so hard to plan!

Because that's what the shower is really all about, isn't it? Capturing the excitement and the fun of her beginning her new life with him. You want your bride especially to have fun, to take some time off from her hectic schedule, and to know how much you love her. You also want to provide a location where she can celebrate with her friends and give everybody a chance to bring her a gift she can enjoy.

Legend tells us that the very first bridal shower was in Holland. A pretty maid fell in love with a miller. Her father, however, didn't want her to marry this guy. Her dad decided to refuse to provide a dowry, hoping to discourage the young couple. But true love prevails! The miller's friends came to the rescue of young love and showered the bride and groom with gifts at the first wedding shower.

Times have changed. Traditionally, bridal showers were a much more meaningful ceremony than they are today. Our grandmothers and their grandmothers really counted on the gifts they would receive. Those gifts helped them set up their new household and embellished whatever dowry their family was prepared to provide. The shower filled out their trousseau. It was critical to a comfortable new life in poorer times that the bride have a shower. Now bridal showers are about giving memories and experiences of love and support, and less about a new bridle for the plough horse or a nice couple of young hens.

Today, the bride's friends, coworkers, or colleagues typically host a wedding shower for a group of the bride's friends to attend. The guests can include men or children or pets or just about anyone or anything you think will be special for the bride. The idea is you want to send her off to the rest of her life with warm memories of her dearest friends.

It's major fun to host a shower, as you are about to discover. It can also be a lot of work. You might find yourself a little overwhelmed by the prospect of planning such an important party in your friend's life. Especially if you aren't accustomed to planning parties yourself. But you'll find everything you need to know here, and together we'll make it easy and fun. You will find handy checklists—whether it's how to track her gifts or a shopping list for the grocery store. You'll find tons of premade sample parties using lots of new, exciting themes. We'll talk about everything from a countdown for the arrangements, to how much food the average person eats at a party, to what colors to use in decorating the location. You will also be glad you found such a complete and thorough companion, and your friends will rave at your success.

By the time this is over, you'll be a pro! You might just find yourself being hired to throw showers in the future for friends of friends! So here's a toast to the bride-to-be, and one to you, for the kindness you're showing by deciding to host her wedding shower.

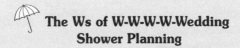

The Ws of W-W-W-W-Wedding Shower Planning

Why are you doing this?
What kind of shower should you have?
Where do you want to have it?
When should you have the shower?
Whom should you invite?

CHAPTER ONE

Wedding Shower Basics

Who Typically Hosts the Shower?

One or more of the bridesmaids, usually led by the Maid or Matron of Honor, are the most typical hosts of the wedding shower, although just about any close friend, neighbor, aunt, cousin, or coworker is perfectly fine, too. You can cohost it if you want with any of these people, or you can do it by yourself.

Who Should NOT Host the Shower?

The people who are *not* supposed to host the shower, according to the etiquette bylaws, are the mother, sister, or grandmother of the bride. However, any of these can hold it at her home, or offer financial contributions to the event. She just is not typically supposed to act as hostess (she doesn't send out the invitations).

She's Got a Bunch of People Who Will Want to Throw Her a Shower

What with work friends and friends from the bride's club, church, school, old family friends, or any one of many disparate groups in a woman's life, chances are there will be plenty of people who want to throw a shower. Probably lots of them don't even know one another. Who's the right one to do it, and how many showers can she have?

That question is answered in many ways. First, are the bride and groom having a big wedding? Are all the people who will be at the shower(s) also invited to the wedding? Is she inviting her whole office staff to the wedding, or just a few people from work?

People who are not invited to the wedding can certainly be invited to a shower. But some wedding-planning books advise the bride not to have shower guests who are not also wedding guests.

Remember that it is redundant and possibly a big financial drain on anyone to be invited to more than two showers for the same bride. With that in mind, it can also make a shower a lot more fun for the bride if groups of people she knows from different parts of her world can meet. Her best friend at work can finally meet Aunt Mabel, about whom she has heard so many stories. It's a kick for some brides to watch this. On the other hand, coworkers might not feel generally comfortable at the family get-together, or their presence there might establish more intimacy with the bride than she feels comfortable with.

For the hostess of the party, the easiest way to resolve this is to ask the bride what she wants. As long as one or two poor souls don't get invited to more than two showers for the same bride, everything will work out just fine. And some of the bride's friends might make new friends with other people who are important in her life.

Do You Want to Do It All Alone? Money Versus Authority Considerations

Let's just assume you want to host the party all by yourself, for whatever reason. You don't care how much work it is, you don't care how much money it costs, you don't care that your house will be trashed after fifteen women leave the party. You just plain want to do it all alone.

OK. You can do it all by yourself, and with all the work will come all the glory and the bride's undying thanks. Cool. But please, consider the following questions before you absolutely make up your mind.

Hosting It Alone Questionnaire

Because even with this book as a helpful guide, it's still a lot of work!

1. Do you have enough time to organize the whole thing?
2. Do you have enough money to pay for the party (a cheap party will cost you about $250)?
3. Do you get excited at the thought of staying up until the wee hours, getting ready the week before the shower?
4. Is your house big enough to hold everyone?
5. Can you cook and bake?
6. Can you afford a caterer?
7. Are you sure there won't be too many wedding showers if you do one?
8. Are you sure nobody will be offended if you do it without their help?
9. How would that make the bride feel if they were upset?
10. Do you like organizing things?
11. Are you great at details?

If you can honestly say yes to most of these questions, you should definitely do it yourself. But there are some benefits to having other people involved:

- Sharing the expenses
- Tapping into someone else's creativity
- Providing a great place to have the shower if they have a bigger house
- Cutting down on the amount of time all this will take you
- Making your life a lot easier while still giving your bride a great party
- Including people you like who cannot or would not do it themselves

If You've Decided to Cohost the Shower, Here Are Some Tips

Cohosting offers lots of benefits, not the least of which are shared expenses and shared responsibilities. You might become great friends (if you aren't already) with whomever you cohost the shower with. You could also want to kill each other, and that tension could mess up the party.

Luckily, you bought this book. Here is the secret to cohosting a fabulous party and having fun doing it. Get ready to commit the secret to memory:

Decide who will do what now, while it's all still a fun theory.

The more you work out now, the easier this whole thing will be for you. The first step is to have a planning meeting with your partner(s). You will want to buy a copy of this book for each of them (my publisher told me to put that in, but it's a good idea), and you will want to copy (and enlarge) the following chart.

Your job at this first meeting with your cohost(s) is to basically decide on a theme and a general idea of who will do what. You probably want to have a meeting with your cohost(s) face to face if at all possible. You will have called the bride already and gotten permission and a couple of possible dates and times she's available.

It's OK if you don't know your cohost(s). Take control of the meeting by showing her how prepared you are. Give her the book and the chart, and after you're done giggling and bonding, choose the date and, ideally, the location and talk about the theme. (If you plan to rent a location, you won't be able to select a place at your first meeting, obviously.)

Delegation Chart/To-Do List

The following form should be filled out and one copy given to each hostess.

Party for:_____

To be held on:_____

Where:_____

From what time to what time:_____

Names of hostesses:_____

Home phone number: _____

work: _____

pager:_____

cell: _____

e-mail: _____

Theme: (choose one from this book or come up with something of your own!)

_____

_____

TASK	PERSON RESPONSIBLE
Invitations:	
Choosing or making them	_____
Buying	_____
Writing	_____
Drawing a map	_____
Mailing	_____
Handling RSVPs	_____
Party Decorations:	
Selecting	_____
Buying	_____
Storing	_____

Delegation Chart/To-Do List (continued)

TASK	PERSON RESPONSIBLE
Assembling	_____
Hanging/decorating	_____
Removing	_____
Menu:	
Choosing the menu	_____
Buying food	_____
Baking/buying cake	_____
Making food	_____
Setting up food	_____
Serving food	_____
Cleaning up kitchen	_____
Location Rental and Setup:	
Selecting a location	_____
Renting a location	_____
Paying the deposit	_____
Preparing a house	_____
Paying for the rental space	_____
Setting up the furniture	_____
Renting the furniture	_____
Returning any rented furniture	_____
Cleaning the house afterward	_____
Removing debris from the rental space	_____
Getting back any deposit	_____

Delegation Chart/To-Do List (continued)

TASK	**PERSON RESPONSIBLE**
Party Favors:	
Choosing party favors	_____
Buying various favors or their components	_____
Assembling party favors	_____
Distributing party favors	_____
Party Games:	
Choosing which games to play	_____
Choosing an entertainer	_____
Paying for an entertainer	_____
Assembling anything necessary	_____
Finding prizes	_____
Buying prizes	_____
Organizing the games	_____
Emceeing the games	_____
Managing the games	_____
Judging the games	_____
Removing or taking down the games	_____
Music:	
Choosing the type of music	_____
Engaging a musician	_____
Paying a musician	_____
Providing CDs or other recordings	_____

Delegation Chart/To-Do List (continued)

TASK	PERSON RESPONSIBLE
Making sure the stereo works well	_____
Changing the music during the party	_____
Making sure the CDs go back to whomever owns them	_____

The Gift Table:

TASK	PERSON RESPONSIBLE
Renting or allocating a gift table	_____
Decorating a gift table	_____
Taking gifts from attendees at the door	_____
Making sure cards stay with attendee's gifts	_____
Recording who gave bride what	_____
Packing all her gifts into big boxes	_____
Putting the big boxes in her trunk	_____
Cleaning up the wrapping paper and ribbons	_____
Assembling the ribbon bouquet for the rehearsal dinner	_____

Then, generally go over the list of things to be done. Make a verbal, out-loud deal to be honest about what your real interests are. Don't sit there like a mouse if you love to bake and would love to make her cake, but you hate picking out music because all you listen to is Old Elvis and everyone teases you about it. Tell your cohost you want to make the darn cake! Pick the jobs you like, let her pick the jobs she likes, and negotiate the rest. Be clear about what you are interested in doing, and what you vehemently DON'T want to do. Chances are, you two can sweet-talk somebody else into doing what you don't want to do or pool your money and hire it done.

At this first meeting, you might also want to talk about money. Who will pay for what is kind of taken care of in the delegation chart, but if you want to do a straight budget, refer to the budget-planning section of this book. A home party can be done for $250 on the very cheap side. From there, the sky's the limit. Reasonably elegant home parties for fifteen people would cost about $400, self-catered, but including the gift you guys give her. Lavish, well, you gotta do some price shopping yourself to discover that one. If you hire Fabio or Pierce Brosnan as a surprise guest, it's going to cost a lot more.

 What to take to your shower-planning meeting with your new cohost(s):

1. A copy of the delegation chart for each host
2. A copy of this book for each host
3. A pen
4. Your personal calendar
5. Your checkbook
6. Your incredible charm and great personality

If You've Decided to Go It Alone ...

Doing it all by your lonesome DOES NOT mean you cannot get all sorts of help with any part you want help with! Including financial aid!

Let's say you want to do it alone, but you want a really cool location—ask another friend, the bride's mom, or somebody else to let you do it at their place. If you can sweet-talk a friend who has a great house but who isn't a friend of the bride's and who would let you use his or her house or yard for the party and maybe not even care to be there him- or herself, you've got a perfect deal!

Know this: The person whose house it is at is usually considered the hostess, no matter what the facts may be, unless the homeowner is a stranger to the attendees. Also, no matter where you are having it, you should psychologically prepare yourself for some breakage. Especially if alcohol will be served. Five percent of even the most perfect parties go wrong—and you just want to make it look like it's all flowing as planned. Never get ruffled, no matter what happens.

The Question is . . . what do you want help with?

- Help with cooking? Do it potluck!

- Help with the cake? Ask one of the attendees who you know loves to bake to make it her shower gift.

- Help paying for it all? Politely ask her or his parents if they'd like to contribute (but know that hers may be already overwhelmed with paying for the wedding), or ask the girls at work to pitch in!

- Help sending out and tracking the invitations? Ask someone with a computer, like a secretary friend who is also a friend of the bride's.

🎁 Help with the party games? You certainly know someone in the group who is always the life of the party and who would love the job.

See? Doing it all by yourself doesn't mean doing it all by yourself. It means you get to practice your skills as a kind and effective manager of others.

Am I Nuts for Doing This Shower?

There could be a moment or two in the next few weeks while you are planning this shower when you think, "Gee, why am I doing this anyway?" Especially if you have never been a bride and had your own shower, if you have small children, if you work full time, if you have anything else to do all day other than plan parties.

You are planning this party because you want everyone to have a memorable time, or a fun time, or for her to know how much you care about her, or because she is your colleague. Or are you also hoping to make new friends? To practice your organizational skills? How about because you wonder if you would like to quit your day job and become a caterer or party planner for a living?

Once you know *why* you want to host this party, you need to think about the kind of person *you* are and the kind of person *she* is. If she's quiet and reserved, she might not

enjoy a party at Chippendale's, even though you and her other friends might. If you or some of the other girls just cannot keep a secret for anything, you might not want to plan her a surprise party.

If you and the bride are friends but your personality styles really don't match, you'll probably want to defer to *her* style as much as possible. After all, this party is for her. Think about the kinds of things *she* loves to do. Would she be more thrilled at an English tea party in a big garden some afternoon? Or a male stripper? Or a traditional party at someone's home or at church? What kind of person is your bride?

If you think about it, you'll come up with all sorts of interesting things she likes to do that might be able to be incorporated into a unique and fun party.

- ✱ Is she a nature lover? Have the party in a national park!

- ✱ Is she a city girl with a love of animals? What about at the zoo?

- ✱ Does she go nuts over Laura Ashley's stuff? You might want to try that tea party in a garden!

- ✱ Is she just a "good ol' girl"? You might have fun at a local pool hall with a surprise male stripper.

- ✱ A Martha Stewart wife-to-be? Try booking a local craft or ceramic shop for some workshop time.

The thing to remember is this: This party should make her feel comfortable and happy. It should not embarrass her or bore her. The idea is a fun night out from all the hectic preparations for the wedding with a bunch of her friends—not a trip to the outer limits of her comfort zone.

What's the Difference Between an Engagement Party and a Wedding Shower?

An engagement party is a party given for the newly engaged couple, often to announce and celebrate their new engagement. It's usually shortly after they get engaged and sort of serves as a public acknowledgement of their commitment to marry.

An engagement party can be formal or informal. Sometimes, when the bride's parents host it, it is a formal sit-down dinner where the couple is toasted and lavished with love and congratulations on their engagement. Gifts may or may not be part of this type of party. Special gifts at this kind of event might include family heirlooms being passed to the new couple. If gifts are included, it's usually considered more of a coed shower than a basic engagement party. A wedding shower has a totally different intent and is usually held close to the wedding.

What's the Difference Between a Bridesmaids' Luncheon and a Wedding Shower?

The bridesmaids either give the bridesmaids' luncheon for the bride, or vice versa. It's a chance for the bride and her friends to hang out together in the hectic days right before the wedding. Usually, nobody else attends. It's usually held on the weekend before the wedding so working girls can get there, too. At this event, the bridesmaids usually give their joint gift to the bride, and she usually gives their individual gifts to them.

The wedding shower, on the other hand, involves all sorts of people, most of whom are not part of the bride's actual wedding party, and it is specifically about giving gifts to the bride.

What If We Cannot Have It Before the Wedding?

If there's absolutely no time before the wedding, it's OK to do it afterward, although this would likely be a coed shower/reception for the couple.

Special Notes for Coworker Showers

The ideal time to have a coworker shower is on one of the last days the bride will be at work before her wedding. Colleagues gather together, often on lunch hour or right after work, and chow down on refreshments (cake, cookies, fruit, tea, soft drinks) and present a group gift.

Special Notes for Church Showers

If you're having a shower for a woman of your congregation, you probably know most of her friends. Unless her other friends and family are of the same faith, though, you might want to reconsider inviting "outsiders," especially if you will be holding it at the church or using any sort of religious rituals during the party. Run it past the bride before you make any final decisions.

Not that you need to be reminded, but some religious groups have particular jargon that could make a few outsiders feel uncomfortable. Think about this and discuss it with your bride. This is NOT the time for making new converts. Further, if the bride is about to have an interfaith marriage and this is any sort of a bone of contention among the couple or their family, please refrain from inviting either his or her womenfolk, as to invite one without the other is rude. If this is the case, you would invite only immediate brethren of the same faith, even if her parents or his are part of your own belief system. The only exception would be if her mother/sister/aunt were an actual member of your local congregation.

If it is customary to pray before each meal in your faith, and the shower is being held in private, please go right ahead. But if it is customary and you are meeting in a public place for the shower, you simply must ask the bride how she will feel about praying in public before you choose to do so. Her choice must be honored. If God/ your Deity is blessing this union, surely He/it will bless you for your love for and consideration of your spiritual sister's emotional comfort.

Special Notes for Club or Sorority Showers

Inviting the other women in your club or group is a given, but please ask the bride if there will also be other wedding showers before the Big Event. If there are not going to be, you have a social responsibility to invite the bride's female family members, as well as the groom's, and probably also her friends from elsewhere, like work or church.

However, if this shower is one of several, or if most of the people who will be at this shower won't or can't be at the wedding anyway, you can certainly leave it to just your group. Ask the bride what she prefers, and, of course, be considerate of her wishes.

Special Notes for Showers for Pregnant Brides-to-Be

If she's expecting her first baby and her first wedding, why not combine the showers into one huge gala event? If it's public knowledge that she's expecting, this could lead to all sorts of fun ideas.

It would be totally appropriate, assuming it's OK with the bride, to have women with children under three show up at this party. Older kids probably ought to stay somewhere else. But hire or lure some teenager to entertain the little ones while you and the soon-to-be-Mommy party. If the bride is totally petrified by the impending motherhood thing, then don't even bother to ask—make it a Big People Only shower and focus on just typical wedding presents.

What If the Groom Has Been Married Before, But She Hasn't?

If it is the groom's second marriage and the bride's first, you need only take into consideration the extent of the groom's possessions. If he already has a fully supplied residence, it would be pointless to have a shower and possibly cause the couple trouble in figuring out whose toaster to put in their now-joint kitchen. You'd want to throw a theme shower if that's the case.

Please note it is certainly acceptable to throw as large and lavish a shower as you desire if it is the bride's first wedding, despite the marital history of her groom.

Getting Married Again— Can We Still Give Her a Shower?

In some cases, it is thought to be in bad taste to have a big wedding or a big shower or more than one shower for a woman who is remarrying. But if the couple-to-be is having a big wedding, there seems to be no logical reason not to have a shower, or more than one, of any size that pleases you and the bride's other friends. Obviously, in the case of a small, private second wedding, it would not be appropriate to have an overwhelmingly large shower. You'll have to use your own judgment.

Further, if the bride and groom already have set up households separately or together, you would not invite people to a shower and expect them to show up with the same sort of gifts they would for a young couple just getting out of school. I suggest you throw a theme party for a second shower—invite the guests to bring something fun and celebrate in the joy of second chances with your bride. Also, it is more typical to have a coed shower in the case of a second marriage.

Special Notes for Showers for Second Marriages

Fifteen years ago, divorce was hushed up. But now that it's open and accepted as part of life, remarriages are entitled to as much hoopla as you and the bride feel comfortable with. While you and the girls probably won't be offering a grown woman new toasters and pillowcases as gifts (refer to the section on gifts for second marriage showers in Chapter 8), there's just as much reason to celebrate the second marriage—and maybe more reason than the first.

A second marriage gives you the opportunity to celebrate the truism that

Remarriage is the triumph of hope over experience
Live it up! Why ever not?

Special Notes for Senior Citizen Wedding Showers

In our wonderful society, people are living longer—and loving longer—than ever before. Isn't this great? A billboard near my home had a picture of a lovely gray-haired bride and groom, about to kiss. The motto of the insurance company who posted the billboard is "There is a plan for every life." I thought the billboard was as touching as it was inspiring.

In the case of a senior shower, there are some basic things to remember that you might not have thought of, especially if you are much younger than the bride. First, make sure everything is easily accessible to people whose ability to walk and climb steps is impaired. Make sure the directions are especially clear, and use 14-point type, 1.5 spaced, to write them. Make sure the parking area is well lit and the house is clearly marked and illuminated. Don't select music you like—select music your bride likes. Don't plan on serving nuts, corn on the cob, or blueberries as crucial choices on the menu. (Dentures hate these items!) Don't plan anything too risqué, unless you think the bride would get a kick out of it. Some of her friends might not.

Show deference by making sure there are plenty of comfortable seats that are easy to get into and out of—both squishy sofas and nice flat-based dining room chairs. Move tottering pedestal end tables and plant stands out of the way, and make sure to leave a wide path between seating areas and the bathroom.

The idea of making senior guests more comfortable is not condescending. Like the sign in the diner—"Don't complain about our coffee. You'll be old and weak yourself someday!" Even if your guests are vibrant, active, and fit, being considerate of the possible needs and potential embarrassment factors for some seniors is gracious of you and in impeccably good taste.

Who Does What?

Ever Wonder What You Are Supposed to Do?

Have fun! After all this work, the party should unfurl close to perfectly! Make sure the food is hot or cold, the drinks don't get too diluted, and no one gets drunk. Other than that, keep people fed and happy and everything will be a masterpiece. You may have discovered a new career option for yourself!

Does the Bride Have Any Responsibilities Before the Shower?

First, before planning a shower, you should ask the bride if she wants you to have it for her. Surprise showers are not ideal for many people, and they are a lot harder for you to plan. Further, the cat almost always gets out of the bag by accident anyway.

If you ask the bride and she says yes, then she is reasonably expected to do the following: She should provide you with a guest list that roughly matches the number of people you want to have. (Which means you have to tell her in advance—the average number is fifteen for a home shower.) She should give you about fifteen to twenty names, because not everyone will be able to make it. It's kind of her responsibility to make sure no one she knows is invited to more than two showers, or it gets to be a drag for the poor guest.

She should also be pretty much OK with the type of shower you want to throw. Unless it's way outside her comfort zone, this should be no problem.

And she needs to tell you the names/locations of the store(s) where she's registered for gifts.

Does the Bride Have Any Responsibilities After the Shower?

A long time ago, she was expected to personally write thank-you notes to each person who attended and gave a gift. But Emily Post has been gone a long time. Now it's totally cool for her to just thank the people who are there, and probably write a brief thank-you to people who couldn't attend but sent a gift anyway.

Also, gosh, a real pal might choose to stay and help you clean up a little, but she's got so many other responsibilities right now that even if she offers, you'll probably urge her to go home and get some sleep. Getting married is the easy part—planning the wedding is the stressful part for most brides. She's probably exhausted.

CHAPTER TWO

Shower Themes

*I*n this section, you'll find all sorts of clever ideas for showers. The ideas are meant to spark your own creativity and give your brain something to chew on. You can always come up with something of your own, or add to the ideas here.

Themed showers are fun for several reasons—the planning is easier; the event is more memorable; the pictures are easy to identify; everyone remembers the event more clearly.

If some of the following stuff sounds too far out, it's no big deal. There are some really conservative ideas tucked in here, too. The idea is that you and your guests and bride have fun and be comfortable. So browse through these lists and pick and choose what you like. Have your cohost select her three favorite themes. You do the same and choose the one(s) that overlaps.

The theme of your party will determine where you have it, of course. Chapter 2, "Shower Themes," will give you plenty of ideas to build on. You can mix and match ideas to come up with something of your own, or it may just spark a fresh idea.

Sometimes, when I am planning a big party, I create it around an object to get a theme. A yellow plastic pineapple bowl I got at an ice cream parlor inspired several Hawaiian parties. Is your couple going to Maui for their honeymoon? You could try to theme your party on their romantic destination, her favorite hobby, something she's always wanted to do (bungee jump? parachute?) or just about anything else.

Think about the other showers you have been to—or ones you two have been to together. What elements did she think were interesting or fun? What kinds of things bring back fond memories of your childhood together, if you knew one another way back then?

The kind of shower you choose will determine *when* you have it, too, as in afternoon or evening, weekend or weeknight. The traditional time to have it is about two weeks before the wedding, but it's even OK two nights before the wedding when the guys traditionally have their bachelor's party. (Two nights allows any hangovers to wear off so the groom is clear-headed when he says, "I do!")

If you think you want to try a surprise party, you should begin to pick a place or time she would least expect. Read the great section on surprise parties at the end of Chapter 2, if you haven't already. Otherwise, and much easier, just call her and ask when would be most convenient, and surprise her with the details. (Which is a much more Day-Timer® way to do it in the very late '90s.)

Once you've given some thought to the *kind* of shower your bride would like most, then you can move on to the next step: choosing a theme. In the following section are some specific questions and answers that might help you focus more clearly before you choose.

Hawaiian Party

For brides-to-be who like Hawaii, who are from Hawaii, who are marrying a Hawaiian, who are going to Hawaii for the honeymoon (the nation's #1 honeymoon destination), or who just like Hawaiian music, this is a perfect idea. If time and weather permit, hold it in the summer, outside. Get lots of flowers and interesting, easily prepared food. Make everyone wear Hawaiian clothes and provide plastic leis when guests arrive (you can get them very cheap from a place called Oriental Trading Company—see address in the back of this book).

Serve fruit punch—spiked and plain—and a main entrée of shish kebabs or sweet-and-sour pineapple meatballs with lots of rice and some Hawaiian bread from the grocery store. See the section on unique invitations in Chapter 5 for a great idea on how to make invitations for this party!

Check out the watermelon basket in Chapter 7. Your local party goods store will be totally stocked for this theme!

A Gala Event

Complete with caterer and rented location, this is an elegant, tasteful, classy party for your chic bride-to-be. Hosted at a local hotel, this party includes men, champagne, a sit-down dinner, and a super cake. Lots of fun, rather pricey, but worth it. Have your guests dress formally or semiformally. See if you can get a band or a harpist to provide live music for the event. For a really clever and elegant invitation, try buying some glossy black paper from the art supply store. With a thin line of glue, write the bride's name or the words "Wedding Shower" on paper you've cut and folded in half. Sprinkle the wet glue with gold glitter. Or get a fancy stamp and a gold glitter stamp pad and stamp the fronts. On the inside, insert a piece of tissue paper in the colors of the shower, or ask the bride if she has leftovers from the invitations. Print the words of the invitation on the inside.

Send each female attendee home with a long-stemmed rose from the table bouquets, or a fancy sachet filled with Jordan almonds in a veil bag tied with gold curling ribbon.

Walk on the Wild Side!

This is her last chance to be a single girl, and the guys are having a bachelor's party anyway, so why not? Hire a male stripper or go to a girls-only dance club. As a party favor, why not provide each guest with a little lacy sachet in which you've tucked a condom and a chocolate kiss? If you don't hire the stripper, you might enjoy the task of interviewing three or four young men from the local college's drama department who would like to act as hosts/waiters for the evening. They could prove invaluable!

You'd probably have the shower in the evening. Replace your entry light with a black-lightbulb, and play your favorite music. You wouldn't want to throw this shower for a demure friend. Have some fun! For the invitations, get some black glossy paper from the art supply store. Cut it so that folded, it fits neatly into your envelopes. On the front of each sheet, cut out a pair of lips, a big X or a big heart. On bright red paper, cut just ¼ inch smaller, print the party invitation. Fold the red in half and insert it into the card so it shows through the cutout on the front of the black. Affix it with a dab of glue in the crease. Very cool!

Western Hoedown

Why not have everyone wear Western wear or even square-dancing costumes? Could you invite guys, too, and hire a square-dance caller and someone to teach y'all in your spacious backyard? How about line dancing? Or do you just want to play Garth Brooks on the CD player and have the guests wear their boots? You'd probably serve a red-meat barbecue—no tofu for this crowd! Or maybe chili, and you could send everyone home with a little package of chili mix.

You could provide everyone with a neckerchief in bright colors—many hobby stores carry them for as little as ninety-nine cents each. You could use a few bales of hay for seating in your backyard.

For clever invitations, buy some brown construction paper, some small chicken feathers (or pull them from a pillow), and a small square of fake leather, leopard skin, or calico fabric. Cut the construction paper into little hat shapes, leaving the top of the hat with a seam so that it opens like a card. Cut the fabric into tiny strips to make hatbands and glue the feathers into the hatband. On the inside, insert the actual wording of the invitation. Yee-haw!

Southwest Fiesta

Not much is easier to cook for a crowd than Mexican food! Whether it's appetizers or a main course, Mexican food is easy to cook, easy to serve, and always popular. Throw some corn chips in a bowl with two or three kinds of salsa (or see the "Do-It-Yourself 12-Step Shower Catering Plan" in Chapter 6 for a great bean-dip recipe). Play Mexican music, decorate with sombreros and serapes (Mexican colorful woven blankets), and hire some mari-achis to come play for your group. You can send the guests home with little loaves of cornbread wrapped in "Mexican"-print fabrics. Don't forget to play some great Mexican music!

For charming invitations, you could make paper flowers out of crepe paper and attach the invitation to the stem. Here's how to do it. You'll want to use 5"×7" envelopes to mail these.

1. Cut six pear-shaped, pear-sized petals for each invitation out of brightly colored crepe paper (from the hobby/craft store). Don't use tissue paper.

2. Roll the petals one by one around a pencil width-wise, from end to end, NOT from the tip of the pearshape to the widest part.

3. Unroll the petals and gather them together at the narrowest part of the shape with a green pipe cleaner in the center. Scrunch them together and wrap some of the pipe cleaner around the petals. This now forms the stamen of the flower and the back of the green pipe cleaner is the stem. Dip this protruding tip into a touch of red paint you've mixed with glue and sprinkle it with green or yellow glitter, or cracked pepper. When dry, attach an invitation printed on heavyweight paper with a hole punched in the corner to the end of the pipe cleaner.

Totally Cool California Shower, Dude!

Is your couple going to California for their honeymoon? Moving there? Coming from there? Why not have a party based on the stereotypes of the West Coast? Offer your guests plastic sunglasses when they arrive, and have them dress Rodeo Drive gaudy or totally beach bum. The food? Heck, that's easy! Serve braised tofu with rice, and a main dish they'll recognize, too. Lots of sprouts, vegetables, whole grain breads, and so on. The drinks must include fruit punch, sparkling water, and smoothies!

Have the party at a local water park or by your pool. Of course, you'll play Beach Boys music! Heck, why not hire a couple of local beach-bum-looking kids to help you serve food and drinks at the party?

Make invitations by sticking contact paper to manila envelopes. Cut them out in the shape of surfboards (like, wow, man!) and paste a printed sheet of data on the "belly" of the board. Totally awesome! You could send your guests home with tiny seashells pressed into white, pink, or blue votive candles you slightly melted. How about little bottles of sunscreen? Beach balls? Totally cool, dude!

Fourth of July/Independence Day Party

Any time is a good time for a Fourth of July party! Is your bride marrying near this holiday? Are either of the couple in the military? Are they going to Philadelphia or D.C. for the honeymoon? Is either of them from there? Is it summer? Does one or both of them realize marriage means a modification of their independence? Can you think of any excuse? The coolest thing about holiday parties is that you can get cheap, cheap, cheap decorations if the holiday has already passed for real. You know what to do—get some firecrackers, dress everything in red, white, and blue.

Obviously, the invitation will have to explain it's the Fourth of July in May, but make clever invitations with silver stick-on stars on blue construction paper with red and white tissue-paper streamers.

Christmas in April/June/July . . . or Even December!

Here's a lovely idea for winter brides, especially if there will be more than one shower, if the shower is coed, or if the shower is for a couple who are entering second marriages.

Theme your party around Christmas! Have everyone bring a Christmas ornament or some other carefully selected holiday decoration for the happy couple. You could give Santa hats to everyone who shows up (which would make for great pictures). Why not hire the Stripping

Santa (for the right crowd), serve eggnog, stack the presents in a sleigh you made out of cardboard, give the guests sugar cookies or gingerbread men as take-home gifts, and decorate the halls with balls of holly!

Of course, your invitation will have to explain the apparently wrong season, if it is. Cute invitations might be two pieces of red-stocking felt sewn together in seconds on your machine, with a white tassel or puff ball on top. Inside, you could insert white triangle-shaped cards with the party info on them. Or what about buying some silk/polyester mistletoe and attaching an invitation to it with a sparkling gold or silver ribbon or wire?

Other Holidays Near the Wedding Day

If there is any holiday at all that's your favorite or the bride's, why not recreate it for the shower? Nobody says we can only have one per year, and decorating for this holiday will be a snap! (Especially if the real one has recently passed!) Thanksgiving, Hanukkah, Kwanzaa, Easter, Lincoln's Birthday, there really isn't anything you cannot do! It will make it easy to decorate and theme, yes, but it could also be a great time for guests who will create fond new memories! If it snows at Christmas in your part of the world, have everyone wear bathing suits and Santa caps to your party in July!

Garden Party

Bring gifts like garden tools, gloves, a kneeling pad, a package of bulbs, a gardening book. Have it outside, serve salads in big clay pots, send the guests home with tiny flowers growing in those precious little 2-inch pots. The cleanup will be a snap—everyone can wear overalls or work clothes. Why not have it at an Arboretum? The ideal invitation would be to send one gardening glove with a hand-shaped invitation inside—guests have to show up to get the other half of their glove as a set! Paint nail polish on the "hand" inside the glove!

Ladies Tea Party

This delightful takeoff on the British tradition of high tea is a charming idea. Serve a true high tea, complete with scones, jam, clotted cream, and an assortment of teas. Have it outside on a big lawn, and have everyone wear tea gowns (usually, some lightweight, summery ankle-length dress).

Perfect if you can find delightful floral tablecloths, some vases of roses and daisies, lace table toppers, and china cups. (Borrow cups from everyone you know who has china!) You could all pitch in for a china service for the bride, or bring tea-related things like a teapot, an assortment of gourmet teas, scone mix, and so forth. Send your guests home with collections of tea bags, tiny pots of jam, bath tea sachets, floral perfume, or potpourri.

I have to admit I am stealing this idea from a batch of cards I saw in England. Clever, delicately patterned heavyweight paper was cut into the shape of a teacup and saucer. The paper was outlined in dark blue so you could immediately recognize it as a teacup and saucer shape. A tiny paper strawberry was pasted to the "saucer" part, and an individually wrapped Earl Grey teabag was tucked into a slit cut in the side of the cup. Adorable! The invitations were printed on the inside.

Wedding Shower by Mail Party

If all of the bride's guests, family, friends, and relatives are far away, here's a cool idea! Have everyone out of town send a present along with a humorous or touching note or memory for the bride. Set up yourself and a few local friends to have the "unwrapping party." Decorate some place and take pictures to send to the folks back home of the bride opening everything. It'll mean the world to those who cannot attend, and the world to your bride.

You would want to send the actual "invitation to send a present" on a piece of sturdy brown cardboard on which you have pasted a smaller printed explanation of what you want them to send. To decorate this invitation, use a bit of jute or even dress it up with a bit of ribbon and a tiny fan-folded spray of wedding gift wrap. Naturally, you will wrap these invitations, and a label preaddressed with your name and address on it, in plain brown paper, slightly oversized, and tie it with jute or twine. Very clever, and it will get the message across. This will probably cost fifty-five cents each to send, however.

At the shower, have the bride or someone read aloud the written memories before opening the packages.

Recipes

Here's a chance to expand your friend's and her new hubby's culinary skills! Have guests write out their favorite recipe and buy the couple of implements necessary for making it. Like a rolling pin and five pounds of pastry flour, a chef's hat and apron, a wok and a bottle of sesame oil, you get the idea. Decorate your walls with fabulous food pictures and get some really interesting things to eat from a variety of cuisines. You could have everyone wear an apron to the shower, or provide them yourself!

You could hire a chef to come give a cooking demo (find one cheap at the local junior college); raffle an Easy Bake or toaster oven for the winner of a party game; supply all the guests with cards to write their recipes and names on and slip them into a plastic photo album for the bride's ease of use; buy her some nice cookbooks; all pitch in and buy a stove or microwave; assign everyone one spice to bring and assemble them on a fancy rack; give away spice sachets to the guests as favors; or surprise the bride with a certificate to a cooking class she wants to attend.

Send recipe cards with the invitation. They could be the preprinted kind with words like "For Pam's Wedding Shower." Dab a drop of cinnamon oil on each card before you slip it into the invitation.

Home Repairs Party

I don't know that I'd do this one unless it's coed, but it is considered a traditional shower. You would suggest that the guests bring things one fixes up a house or yard with. Gardening gloves, rakes, paint brushes, a drill, things like that.

You could also bring books on the subject, a discount coupon from a handyman, a gift certificate to a paint store, or have one of those ladies who sells home decorating out of a van come and do a demo (pay her on the side and be clear about whether or not she can pitch her wares during the party).

For food, you could use paint-roller pans (new, clean ones!) as serving dishes, have everyone wear a painter's cap with his or her name on it (a cheap, easy way to learn new names!), and have everyone dress in overalls. Or you could have the shower at the bride-to-be's new house and everyone could really pitch in! Send the guests home with garden trowels or paint brushes tied with ribbons.

Perfect invitations would, of course, be to buy a really inexpensive set of aluminum pocket screwdrivers—those little ones not bigger than 3 inches, with brightly colored plastic handles. You could tie them securely to sturdy paper invitations with a bit of twine or wire, so they won't slip during mailing and make holes in the envelope or stab the mailman! Short of that, what about mailing cheap plastic switch-plate covers with printed invitations glued to the inside?

Paper

Guests bring stationery, casual home dining stuff (like paper plates), Christmas wrapping paper, toilet paper, a subscription to the local paper, anything paper! This theme also works with wood, glass, metal, vinyl, plastic, and so forth. Make sure to decorate with luminarias, those Mexican lanterns made from waxed paper bags, or Chinese lanterns. Give the guests who come a special mock-up of a newspaper showing the bride and groom on a fake front page, talking (thank God for mail merge) about the special friendship they have with that guest. (Ask the bride for helpful stories.) Take Polaroids of the party and slip them into store-bought paper frames as a giveaway for guests or a keepsake for the bride.

If you have time, a lovely invitation for this would be to take several different types and textures of paper and crinkle them, tear them, and paste them onto heavy white paper. Spray them with setting spray (craft store) and then iridescent glitter spray.

Make the House a Home

Ask each guest to bring a gift for a particular room of the house, such as bathroom, bedroom, living room, kitchen, garage, and so forth. Obviously, you can overlap if you have more guests than rooms. Place the wrapped gifts in the appropriate rooms of your house and have guests migrate with the bride while she unwraps them. You're in for some great photo opportunities! Shape your invitations like little houses, or stick a Monopoly house to each one. Bake a cake or have one made that is shaped like a house (or has a plastic one or a picture of one on it). Make up a plaque that says "Home Sweet Home" for the newlyweds to hang, and give each guest a marker to sign it. Send your guests home with those cute little tiny clay pots filled with a small plant, candies, or a fake topiary.

Use Monopoly money as invitations, or send invitations tied to a brick, or just cut little houses out of construction paper and use different textures and colors of paper and fabric to create the siding and roof of the house.

Pamper Yourself

Here's where you and the other guests pamper yourselves at the shower. Have it around your pool, or at a day spa, where you can isolate for the day. Or, to keep costs down, hire a manicurist, a beauty consultant, even a Mary Kay specialist who can teach proper makeup application techniques. Set up a long table in your living room with mirrors and pots of colors and pretend you're all in high school again experimenting with makeup and different looks.

Or better yet, hire a masseur or two—preferably the buff, tanned young male type, to come give everyone a massage at the party! Let your guests wear sweats or bathrobes and just have a "Girls Day Off" time. Send everyone home with a little bottle of bath oil.

Attach the invitations to little bottles of ninety-nine-cent nail polish. Or else get decorative plastic bags—like gift bags for kids' parties—and stuff them full of cotton balls. Insert a brightly colored invitation shaped like a hand or a foot into the center of the bag and seal it. Mail them in large envelopes.

Guests bring gifts of self-pampering for the bride—a gift certificate for a facial or manicure, a husk pillow, a terry-cloth robe, flannel jammies, a bottle or two of nail polish.

His and Hers

Guests bring items the couple can use together—a bottle of fine wine, his-and-hers monogrammed towels, CDs, and so forth. This is usually a coed affair. Appropriate games for couples would be played, as well as raffling off a dinner for two at a local restaurant, and so on. A barbecue would be the perfect meal to compliment a his-and-hers shower. You might want to arrange dancing on your lawn or in your living room, and you would have the bride and groom sit beside one another and take turns opening gifts.

Make invitations by cutting big initials for their first names out of pretty, sturdy paper.

Glue the initials to the front of slightly smaller cards and trim to fit envelopes. Take some glitter glue (craft store) in a bold contrasting color and make a swath across the front. When it dries, attach printed-out information to the inside.

Bottle and Bar

For this party, guests would bring things to help the couple set up their home bar: glassware, liquor and wine, coasters, trays, shaker, ice buckets, and so forth. Perhaps a book on drink mixing? (Look for the *Everything Book of Bartending* at a bookstore near you!) Everyone could pitch in to get them something really great—like a wonderful blender.

Could you hire a local bartender to come teach people how to make exotic drinks? If you do this "girls only," would you like to hire some handsome waiters to serve? You'd probably do this party in the evening, and perhaps without a meal but with hors d'oeuvres. Send the guests home with tiny alcohol bottles tied with ribbon that matches the party decorations.

For the best possible invitation to this shower, buy those little champagne bottles that are party favors—the ones where you pull the string and the confetti shoots into the air. Tie heart-shaped paper invitations to them and mail them. They'll be bulky but adorable. Mail them in 5"×7" manila envelopes.

Honeymoon

Gifts for this party would be travel items for the couple-to-be to use in their planned destination. Things like travel alarm clocks (or maybe not?), a camera, luggage, small leather goods, guidebooks, and so on. Decorate the room with travel posters. Send invitations that look like tickets.

Put a palm tree or a little Big Ben clock or something else appropriate on the cake, and serve food reminiscent of the region to which they will travel.

You could ask a bunch of people to provide slides, images, pictures, or video of the location or even write to the tourism board for a travelogue segment (not more than fifteen minutes long!). You could make it funny by doing a voice-over of your wedding couple's imaginary trip and first night together.

Paris? Try mailing paper French flags as invitations. The grand tour of Europe? You'd make friends by mailing small Toblerone chocolate bars to everyone, with the invitation attached. Maui? Mail tiny doll-sized grass skirts you made from green tissue paper with miniature bras you cut from floral-patterned fabric tied to an invitation shaped like a woman's torso. Florida? Send paper orange invitations dabbed with a drop of orange oil.

Wishing Well

This shower could also be considered an activity. A wishing well shower is a throwback to older times when the couple was first setting up house. In addition to a regular present, the guests are asked to bring some small item such as a spatula, a potholder, a sponge, a washcloth, a spool of thread, or a box of lightbulbs. The guests wrap the gifts themselves and tape a handwritten poem or note to them.

The hostess builds or buys something similar to a wishing well and ties a length of ribbon to each gift. The bride pulls the objects out of the wishing well and reads the poems one by one. This is an amusing diversion and may be a lot more enjoyable than a typical shower game. A variation would be risqué gifts or sexual implements, but only when the attendees are all about the bride's age. No heart attack for Granny!

Send the guests home with little gifts of their own, like seed packets, small screwdrivers, wooden spoons tied with ribbons, and so on. Your invitations would probably be little wishing-well shapes, easily made from wood-grain contact paper adhered to manila folders and cut out.

Service

Rather than bringing gifts, everybody shows up with a service to be provided after the couple-to-be returns from their honeymoon. This can be a service they either provide or purchase. Things like cooking a meal for them, helping unpack, offering to return yucky wedding presents, and so on. Services that one might pay for would be a week of maid service, a dry-cleaning service, some sort of handyman time for a specific number of hours, and so forth.

You could give your guests as a party favor a coupon or invitation to a "Welcome Back Mr. and Mrs. Jones" party to be held a week or two after the bride and groom return. So cute!

Make your invitations look like coupons, too, with dotted "cut here" marks. Microsoft Publisher could create this in seconds for you—it has a great template.

Entertainment

Things to entertain the new couple might include a movie, pitching in to get them a VCR, CDs, a movie gift certificate, tickets to a local show for the two of them, a magazine subscription, and best-selling books. Rent a few old movies to watch with lots of popcorn. Put up posters of old movies, take a lot of pictures, stuff like that. Show the bride's favorite movie?

Send the guests home with gift certificates from Blockbuster, a bottle of CD-cleaning fluid tied with ribbon, or a popcorn ball.

For great invitations, cut out a couple of pictures of movie or music people from *People* or a similar magazine. Glue one head to the front of each of your invitations. Put a little cloud (like in a comic strip) above each of their heads: "_____, will you be at Veronica's

(their name)

wedding shower? I wouldn't miss it for the world!"

Cary Grant Special

What fun! Gather up the girls and load up on sappy old movies, root beer floats, and pizza! Give everyone a small package of tissues as a party favor. Pop the lenses out of cheap plastic sunglasses and make '60s cats-eye glasses by gluing some silver glitter to the outer edges of the frames.

Go on the Internet and download Cary's picture. Make copies of it, or one of his movie posters, and use them as covers on your invitations.

Gone with the Wind

Frankly, Scarlett, your friends won't want to go home! Watch the movie after having a picnic or luncheon on the lawn, complete with big floppy Scarlett hats you decorated yourself, or that you have your guests decorate as a project. You can buy tiny hats, 4 inches in diameter, at the craft store. Use these as invitations, or fill them with potpourri and seal them with lace circles hot-glued in place and give them as party favors.

You will, of course, need to serve mint juleps and iced tea and have plenty of flowers around. Would you all like to wear Scarlett dresses for the occasion?

Ceramics Studio (or stained glass, knitting, or some other craft where the guests all take home their own handmade "souvenir")

If you or the bride are into some interesting hobby, why not have the party at a studio? From there, guests can go eat in a local restaurant and open presents there. The object they create becomes their party favor. It could convert a lot more people to a craft or hobby your bride and you already enjoy together.

If you are renting a place that commonly holds parties, they may provide invitations for you. Otherwise, why not send a colorful plastic paintbrush skewered through the front of an invitation shaped like an artist's palette.

Wilderness Trek

What could be more fun for your outdoorsy bride and you than to do a "girls only" campout some weekend before the wedding? Of course you'll eat s'mores and tell ghost stories, but you could also theme the gifts to things she'll use when she and her honey go camping. This might be the perfect chance for you all to relax and just have fun one last time without the guys.

For fun invitations, find yourself a piece of bark (elm would be good and not heavy) and glue some dried wildflowers to it along with your invitation—printed, of course, on recyclable paper.

Road Trip

Pretend you're teenagers again! Gather a gaggle of girls, pile into someone's car or van, and head off for a local hot spot. Maybe your destination will be a town not too far away from where the bride's from, or where there are other friends to host you all. Spend the weekend remembering, playing, laughing, and just being girls. For gifts, you could all chip in and have something sitting in her front yard or living room when you all get home. How about a microwave or a new washing machine? You could even make your invitation from foil and paper to look like a road sign.

Ski Party

Right in your own backyard! Wear big woolly sweaters, light a fire, and roast marshmallows, just like in the lodge. The gifts could be things she'll need to learn to ski, ski gear, tickets for lessons, or coupons for lodges or even ski passes. You'll serve hot chocolate and maybe all hang out in the Jacuzzi afterward and reminisce.

Get some knit fabric and cut tiny sweater shapes. Get some wood-grain paper or contact paper stuck onto lightweight cardboard and cut out skis. Hot glue first the skis, then the sweater, to the front of your invitations. Cute! Send your guests home with packets of hot chocolate mix you decorated.

Nifty '50s Party

Let's go to the hop! Turn your kitchen into a do-it-yourself malt shop, complete with hamburgers. Remove your furniture and your shoes. Invite the guys—or don't invite them!

Wear poodle skirts, hire a DJ, and have a dance! You provide neckerchiefs or bobby sox for the girls. Offer a bowl of fake tattoos for the young toughs; serve bubble gum cigarettes. For great invitations, take a regular paper napkin and frill the edges out by scalloping them with scissors. On very cheap white paper, print out the party directions. Insert it into the paper napkin you cut and crinkle it like a waitress in a diner might have a crinkled handkerchief in her name pin in the '50s. Then, tie a knot with curling ribbon. Write the would-be guest's name on a piece of cardboard you might have even decorated, like the waitress's pin, and hot glue it to the knot in the curling ribbon.

Slumber Party

When's the last time you went to a slumber party? Remember when you were little girls? Have you known the bride since you two really were having slumber parties? Make this the complete thing—with sleeping bags you rented, toenail polish, chocolate, popcorn, and ghost stories. Gifts could be things she'll use in the bedroom. Make invitations out of little pieces of fleece or fake fur cut into the size of hotdog buns, sewed together (quickly) inside out (fuzzy on the inside; the outside of the fabric forms the outside of the sleeping bag). Stick the long, body-shaped paper invitations into the sleeping bags.

Appliances Party

In the best version of this party, everyone contributes to buying an appliance the new couple needs, and you have it delivered by some burly young men during the party. But, you could also have guests

buy small appliances for the couple. (Watch the guests' expenses here—they may have planned a small appliance as a wedding gift.) If the new oven is already set up in the living room when the bride gets there, you could open the door to pull out the shower cake. If your appliance is a dryer or washer, you could open it up to reveal that it is stuffed with the packages of washable clothing items your guests brought. Cute idea, huh?

Send everyone home with refrigerator magnets, or use them as invitations. Or, you could go to the appliance store, get a bunch of Maytag tags (especially ones with that bored serviceman on them), and mail them on your invitations.

Toga Party

Remember how much fun this was in college? A few simple bed sheets, some pins, and you're all set to party. You might like to invite the guys to this one. Make your guests wear laurel-leaf wreaths on their heads, just like Julius Caesar did. You can make them out of wire and leaves you buy at the crafts or silk flower store. For the bride and groom, spray paint them gold. Serve Greek food. Include some baklava with the cake, or send your guests home with some wrapped in pretty gold foil.

Great invitations would be to cut some off-white linen paper stamped with a gold "Greek" border. You can probably find a rubber stamp with this pattern, or you can cut the shape out of potato (in relief). Really, potatoes make good stamps, and you can surely get the ink at the stamp store in the mall.

Egyptian Party

You all dress like the toga party, but rent a Cleopatra outfit for your unsuspecting bride. She has to wear the Cleopatra wig, too. Make arm bracelets for your guests out of gold fabric-covered wire (crafts store) or electrical wire spray-painted gold (building-supply store). Wear sandals, do it outside, and don't forget to play the song "Walk Like an Egyptian."

Decorate your table with reeds and palm fronds; scatter some sand. Send out invitations that have gilt edges, and paste a palm frond onto the cards. (Get small palm-frond-looking silk plant leaves at the crafts store or silk floral supply store.)

Give a prize to the best costume. If you're really creative, you could come up with a lot of quips about the bride being in "De Nile" about the realities of married life.

Costume Party

Why not invite the guys, too, and turn this into a real festive event? Make everyone come as a famous couple from history—Romeo and Juliet, Henry VIII and Anne Boleyn, Anthony and Cleopatra, Frankenstein and his bride, and so on. Make sure you either rent a costume for the bride and groom or tell them in advance!

If you want to turn it into a masquerade party, everyone would wear masks until midnight, when they would remove them all at once and discover at last who is who! You might choose to provide the masks for this, as party favors.

Exciting invitations would be to cut mask shapes (like the Lone Ranger's) from black paper. Use glitter glue and feathers to decorate the mask and write the details on the back.

Books Party

What a great idea! Go to the local bookstore and find out which authors are local. Call them or their agents and have one or more of them come to read on the topic of their

book(s) (love, marriage, sex, dating, comedy, etc.). You might pay them a few bucks, or you might let them sell copies of their book(s) at the party. Better, buy their book(s) at a discount in advance from them or the bookstore (the discount from the publisher to you direct would be

40 percent or more). Let them read excerpts. Lots of authors have a great sense of humor and teach on their subject anyway, so you might want to investigate someone local who writes on what the bride is interested in.

Of course, perfect invitations would be bookmarks, book-shaped invitations that open. Party favors could be $5 gift certificates to the local bookstore. (See the section on getting prizes donated in Chapter 11.)

Dr. Ruth Party

There are plenty of Dr. Ruth impersonators in the country. You can find one for the party. Find a novice one by calling a speakers bureau in your area, or you can get a friend who is good with voices to write a script. If your impersonator looks like Dr. Ruth, she can show up at the party. If she doesn't, have her call in during the party to talk to the bride. Put it on speakerphone. Have her embarrass the hell out of the bride. If you cannot find your own Dr. Ruth, contact ForthWrite Speakers Bureau at 310-457-5785 and ask for Wendy Keller. (She's an agent who books performers.) You could also have Sally Jesse Raphael, Bill Clinton, Abe Lincoln, Joan Rivers, you name it! Have Dr.

Ruth offer your poor bride sex advice. Have her take questions from your guests and offer hilarious advice.

Dance Class Party

Have the shower at the local Arthur Murray studio—you'll all be glad if there's dancing at the wedding reception. Learn how to polka, fox trot, disco, or ballroom dance together! Or you can even learn the Macarena! After you're all done learning to dance, head over to a local ice cream parlor and open the presents on the grass outside while you lick your ice creams and laugh. Make sure to take a camera to the lessons! It would be a lot cheaper than you think, and very little work!

Or, you could hire a dance instructor to come to your house. Maybe even a cute dance instructor who teaches in his G-string? And begins by teaching the bride how to shimmy?

Send your guests home with a pair of ballet shoes, a maraca, finger cymbals, something appropriate. The perfect invitation? A paper cutout of a vinyl record, or a paper cutout pair of dance shoes.

'70s Again

Everyone dresses like the '70s and grooves to some slick tunes. Rent a 'fro wig or two to play with! Those ghastly clothes are everywhere now—you can get them cheap at a local thrift shop. There are plenty of '70s composite music CDs around—you could buy them for the party and then give them away as party favors at the end. (That way, you wouldn't embarrass yourself by keeping them!)

Serve '70s canapés like Cheez Whiz, peanut butter and jelly sandwiches, Good & Plenty—all the tacky stuff you can remember.

Elvis Commemorative

Love me tender, baby! Watch one of his movies, play his songs, and even hire an impersonator—Lord knows there are enough of them! Maybe you could turn this into a dance? Would you serve food like in the '70s-themed party to commemorate the King's passion for quality food items? Award a pair of suede shoes, any size, you got at the thrift store and spray painted blue, to the winner of your dance contest. The party favors could be licorice records. Spray little plastic baby shoes first with Christmas flocking, then with blue paint, and attach little cards that say "Thank you . . . Thank you very much!"

For easy invitations, download his picture off the Internet, but I have a better idea. Buy a ½ yard of white polyester fabric, some gaudy rhinestones, and a studding machine (total cost under $10). Impress some rhinestones into the polyester, cut up the fabric into small pieces, and slip the pieces into sealed plastic bags. Attach a laser-printed note that says, "Genuine Piece of Elvis's Costume, circa 1968, Estimated Value $1200—*Sotheby's.*" Send the sealed bags with a handwritten note allegedly from Elvis, personally announcing that he's about to reappear just for the shower.

Flowers Party

Do it at your local arboretum, with a lecture on gardening. Have everyone bring a pottable perennial along with her gift. Give guests packets of seeds with little trowels as remembrances. Raffle off gardening gloves. Give a gift certificate to the local nursery, or have someone from the nursery come lecture on various plants that grow well in your area. Have guests wear flowers in their hair or wear dresses with flowers on them. Get plates and cups that have flower designs and serve salads out of big flowerpots you wash and give to the bride. See the Garden party for clever invitation ideas.

Balloons Party

Stuff your house with balloons, hire a person who makes balloon animals to float amongst your guests (as favors), then shuttle everyone off to the local balloonist launch pad for a real hot air balloon ride! Your cake, decorated like a hot air balloon, could say "Up, Up, and Away—Good Luck Cathy!" Make sure you hire enough balloons to give everyone a ride—or call the local balloonists' club and see if they'd like to help you out. You can fit only about three passengers in a balloon. And make the ride the last part of the party.

You could give guests helium balloons with mesh canopies and ribbon ropes holding Dixie cups full of nuts or M&Ms or something as cute favors. For invitations, attach a few brightly colored deflated balloons to cardboard.

Picnic in the Park

You can figure this one out all by yourself! Play old-fashioned picnic games and bring the kids if the bride has them, too. Give the guests red gingham fabric napkins, and buy the bride an awesome picnic basket as a gift.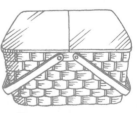
Have everyone bring a gift and a small non-perishable food item that they can picnic with. Send invitations written on red-and-white gingham paper plates.

Chocoholics Party

From the plates to the food to dessert, do it with chocolate! If you want something done right, you have to do it with chocolate, right? If you don't already know how to make molded chocolate candies all by yourself, go to the Wilton Cake Shop in your city, or at JC Penney's, and learn how. Plan a decadent cake, make sure someone brings the bride a gift of chocolate edible underwear, and you're all set!

Attach an Andes mint to each invitation, or a Hershey's Kiss, but only if you will be mailing them in cool weather.

Linens Party

Find out in advance where the bride has her linen registry. Then have everyone bring a linens item. Everything from sachets for the linen closet, to White Linen perfume, to Queen-sized flannel sheets would be welcome. You and your guests might like to cross-stitch or even fabric paint some dish towels together as a project.

Send the guests home with potpourri sachets (see Chapter 12, "Party Favors"). The perfect invitations would be little 1" × 2" pillows you made yourself out of fabric snippets, scraps of lace, and fiberfill. Short of that, how about cutting out bed shapes from cardboard and hot gluing to them a tiny fabric bedspread you have to lift to read the invitation?

Quilting Bee

This is a charming, old-fashioned way to have a wedding shower. You'd want to make sure most of the quilt was done before the shower, because you cannot do the whole thing in one evening. Set up a quilting bee of women who can or will use a needle properly. Give the result as a collective gift to the bride. You'll probably have to hire someone to design it, finish it, or start it before. Set the quilt out on a big table (ask at the fabric store how it's done properly) and have everyone bring their reading glasses and a thimble.

Adorable invitations would be to have a piece of fabric (preferably with a quilt print on it) skewered with a quilting needle. Spools of thread or a gift certificate from the fabric store would make a delightful shower favor.

Wine and Cheese Party

Is there a local winery near you that would love to host this? If not, do it at home. It's elegant and simple. Get a connoisseur to help you if you don't already know what to select. Have several types of wine and cheese and some good crackers and breads. Hire some real waiters. Make everyone come black tie—no matter where it is. Get a harpist or a violinist or play chamber music. Very classy.

Send folks home with airline-sized wine bottles wrapped in gold mesh and tied with colored curling ribbon. Ideal invitations would be fake wine labels from the Vineyard of Mr. and Mrs. _____ (whatever the new couple's name is).

Housewife Party

What fun! Everybody wears fuzzy slippers, bathrobes or aprons, and hair rollers and mud masks! Get a more theatrical-minded guest to show up with a large pregnancy under her dress (a big balloon). Have your guests go home with a can of Ajax with a bow on top as a party favor. Award a pair of bunny slippers to the winner of your biggest contest. I don't think I'd invite the guys to this one. Give the bride a book on how to clean anything, and arrange a bouquet of feather dusters on the table. Have the bride sit in a special chair, from which she "rules" with her toilet bowl brush scepter.

The greatest invitations would be rolled up, scroll-like, and stuffed inside big pink plastic hair rollers.

Amusement Park Party

Go just have fun and pretend you're kids at the local amusement park! Or a carnival! Open presents at your house first, with hamburgers off the grill. Give everyone a free roller coaster ride or something little as a party favor. Draw clown faces on your invitations with markers and glitter glue.

Japanese Party

Decorate your house in the traditional Japanese party style, with paper lanterns and cushions on the floor around a low table. Or hire a room at the local Japanese restaurant. Serve sushi, rice, and cashew chicken or snow peas, or just order in the food. Give everyone a pair of chopstick-like hair skewers. Have a kimono ready for the bride. Float lotus or even magnolia blooms in low dishes of water.

How very Zen of you to write your invitations on gray rice or vellum paper with a Japanese font or calligraphy or even a bit of brush painting. Or you could send them as origami.

All-American Party

Just do the traditional thing—serve cake, coffee, and plenty of gossip and laughter. This is the most common type of shower, where you just hang out for a few hours with the girls. Nothing fancy is needed, it's very casual, and it just sort of happens, without a real theme.

Surprise Parties!

A surprise party! What a wonderful idea! All you have to do is coordinate a time when your bride has absolutely nothing planned; keep at least fifteen people from leaking your secret to her; and figure out who should be invited, where the bride is registered for gifts, and what she wants most from the shower. Not that hard, is it?

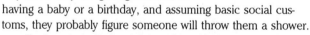

In my experience, very few brides (or for that matter, birthday girls or mothers-to-be) are actually surprised by their shower. After all, they know they are getting married, or having a baby or a birthday, and assuming basic social customs, they probably figure someone will throw them a shower.

Further, it really is tricky getting people not to talk about it to the guest of honor! Most people will be great at keeping the secret, but there's always one who apologetically says, "Linda, I'm so sorry I won't see you Thursday night! I have to. . . ." And then they see the surprised look on Linda's face (the same one she'll have to fake at the actual shower!) and say, "Well, I mean, I *had* been thinking we should get together for dinner some night before your wedding, and I'd kind of chosen this Thursday without telling you, and well, now I just cannot keep this dinner plan we actually never had" or some sorrier rendition of the same. But if you absolutely insist on having a surprise shower, this section will help you handle it as flawlessly as possible.

First, your main objective is to get together a guest list that will include everyone the bride wants to invite. The easiest way to do this is to ask her best friends (if you aren't the best friend), the local girlfriends, or the groom. In fact, the absolutely best way is to ask each of them to come up with a list of twenty people they think should be invited, and then check for overlap and invite all the people on the lists.

Now, you have to figure out where she's registered for gifts. For this, ask her or her Mom (if you really want to be sneaky). Make sure to include registry information on the invitations so the guests don't have to guess what the bride's tastes are.

Next step is finding a way to contact all these people. You are likely to get things as vague as "I know she has a friend named Jackie who works in the office next door to hers." Finding these people will require more than a little ingenuity on your part. But be persistent: you wouldn't want to leave out anyone that might be meaningful to the bride.

On the invitations, set the start time at half an hour before your bride is due to come. This way you ensure that even the stragglers aren't walking up the drive at the same time she is and thus ruining everything. You might want to say, "DEBBIE ARRIVES AT 7:30, so PLEASE show up at 7!" on the invitations.

Once you have assembled a decent guest list, you need to take extra precautions to make sure no one who is invited to the party spills the beans. Mark the outside of the envelopes "TOP SECRET" in big red letters, or write on the invitation "SSSSH! This is a surprise party!" You want to remind them on the map and so forth so that they will feel totally guilty if they screw up and ruin the surprise.

Make sure the bride can show up on the day you select. The easiest way to make this happen is to enlist the aid of someone she knows will NOT be throwing the shower to arrange a "date" with her the night of the shower. It is commonly the groom who acts as the decoy, but it could be another girlfriend or her mom. You simply get this person to ask her out to dinner on the day and at the time you want to hold the shower. Make sure the event they invite her to would require people to be dressed similarly to the way your shower guests will be dressed so that she is not uncomfortable. She should not be the only one prepared to go roller blading at your English Tea Garden party.

On the day of the shower, call the decoy an hour before the scheduled arrival and ask if they are on schedule. Remember, the bride has a lot of details to handle, and she could be running a little late for myriad reasons. Make sure the guests park their cars away from the house. Tell the decoy to take a circuitous route to the location if it isn't a public or rented facility.

Turn out the lights and be prepared to flick them on and swing open the door when she walks inside ahead of the decoy. Get the rest of the guests settled and ready to yell "surprise" as she walks into the room.

As hard as it sounds, the payoff is huge. Everyone who says that he or she hates surprise parties in truth loves the attention and the real message behind the party. That they are special enough to warrant all this extra effort.

CHAPTER THREE

Show Me the Money

How to Budget the Shower

N ow that you've decided on a theme, the next step is to set a budget. Throwing a shower is lots of fun until you start to total all the receipts. Then you find out that the extra $5 there and the extra ten cents each here somehow added up to more than you wanted to spend. And then you'll feel bad because you put yourself in an uncomfortable financial position by spending more than you had allotted in your personal budget. You might find yourself begrudging all the work you did and money you spent.

If the idea of budgeting makes you queasy, or if you bought into the myth that "girls aren't as good with numbers," relax. Budgeting a shower is easy, and you can use the same principles to budget the rest of your life, if you are so inclined. As for "girls aren't good with numbers," bah-humbug! Just wait and see what a genius you are, using this simple system.

The first step is to decide how much money you can spend on this shower. Not about, but exactly. (Exactly makes it easier.) If money is no object, great. Make a budget anyway, so that it all comes out evenly and you know in advance what it will cost you.

You already know you can save money by making things yourself. As you read through this book, you'll see many clever ways you can cut corners and still throw a nice party. You can negotiate with the caterers, with the bakery, and with the rental location. You can get other people to bring things; you can get other people to send you checks. You can ask local businesses to contribute a coupon for dollars off certain services or goods, like meals, to provide you with raffle items or prizes for shower games. The only true limit on your wallet is your creativity. You can have the most wonderful party, if you are willing to supply a little elbow grease!

Now, if you're thinking, "How can I know how much I will spend if I don't know how much it will cost?" let me give you a few ballpark figures:

A cheap at-home shower without a meal will probably run you under $100.

An at-home shower with a simple but elegant meal will probably come in around $250.

A catered event at a restaurant with or without live music will probably cost you about $50 per person, all inclusive.

For example, let's take the costs of a shower I'd plan with food in my home for fifteen women in California—$325. That works out to just over $20 a head. You will now allocate the money based on the Budget Planner.

First, write in the amount you have to spend in the first column. Then, going down the list, you will see the various things you can spend this money on. Spending more in one category obviously leaves you less for others.

Ask yourself and your cohost, "What's most important to us?" On the line provided before each item, rate the items in order of importance to you in pen. If it's more important to you to have great food than to rent a space, mark that first. If you really have to have live music, but you could care less about the decorations, mark that. There's no right or wrong, this is your shower, although you should try to think about the bride's preferences.

Now you'll have a great idea about what's important to you. If you wanted to spend all your money on just decorations, you could certainly find a way to do it! And would they ever be grand! But, of course, everyone would be starving.

Budget Planner

What I want to spend: $_____

	ESTIMATED COST	ACTUAL COST
Invitations:	_____	_____
Postage:	_____	_____
Number of guests:	_____	_____
Rental space:	_____	_____
Decorations:	_____	_____
Flowers:	_____	_____
Food:	_____	_____
Cake:	_____	_____
Drinks:	_____	_____
Entertainment:	_____	_____
Party favors:	_____	_____
Party games:	_____	_____
Present for bride:	_____	_____
Music:	_____	_____
Photography:	_____	_____
Video recording:	_____	_____
Cleanup afterward:	_____	_____
Total:	_____	_____

You are going to allocate some money for each of the items you marked as important to you.

You can probably guesstimate what the most expensive items will be, especially based on what you really want. So in pencil—and please use pencil!—write down how much you would like to estimate for each item. Start with your highest-priority item and work down your list in the order you ranked the items.

If the sum doesn't equal the number on top, work it again until it does. Here's why: You can pay a bakery $40 for a shower cake, you can pay $14 for it at the grocery store, you can bake it yourself for about $8, or you can get someone to bake it, possibly for free. If cake is high on your priority list, $40 or $14 would be a good number, wouldn't it? But if cake is low, then free or $8 would be better. See how it works?

Every number you write down, you can find the same or similar things cheaper, or you can make them yourself. You can also find things that are more expensive.

Once you have your numbers sorted out, you're ready for the actual shopping. As you shop, some things will catch your eye, and you may readjust your priorities. Some things may cost more or less than you thought. Keep a running total of your actual expenses in the column at the right. Keep the receipts in a Ziploc plastic bag that is paper-clipped to your budget.

To be really, really precise about this, you could take the $325 in cash and place some of it in envelopes marked with the words "cake," "music," "cleanup," and so on. Then, when the time comes to pay for the item, you just open the envelope, pay the bill in cash, and put the change in a miscellaneous envelope. I know several people who run their household budgets this way.

Budget Planner

What I want to spend: $325

	ESTIMATED COST	ACTUAL COST
Number of guests:	15	14
Invitations:	$5	$3 (made myself!)
Postage:	$4.80	$4.80
Rental space:	$0	$0 (at home)
Decorations:	$60	$46 (found discount store)
Flowers:	$20	$22 (assembled myself)
Food:	$75	$78 (partially catered)
Cake:	$20	$14 (grocery store)
Drinks:	$10	$9 (mix from party store)
Party favors:	$10	$14
Party games:	$10	$6 (got raffle donation)
Present for bride:	$40	$52 (silk peignoir)
Music:	$14	$0
Photography:	$12	$12
Video recording:	$0	$0
Cleanup afterward:	$40	$38
Total:	$320.80	$298.80

I'm a Bit Low on Funds for This Shower. Who Can Help Me?

If you want to be the hostess but are short of funds (or just need some help with all the details), it's perfectly OK and even welcome to invite the bridesmaids to participate financially, even if they cannot attend the shower for some reason. The bridesmaids traditionally pool their resources for the shower, led by the Maid or Matron of Honor. Other people to invite to participate financially are the mother, sister(s), grandmother(s), and even the future mother-in-law of the bride.

 Ways to Save Money

- Do more of it yourself
- Recruit others to do things for you
- Get someone to help you pay for it
- Solicit money from attendees
- Have it at home

CHAPTER FOUR

Choosing a Venue

The Pros and Cons of Having It at Your House

Having it at your house gives you plenty of flexibility and saves you money. You have the benefit of not having to travel, on top of any other things you may have to do in the line of your wedding-shower duties. You can decorate it and store food items any time you please.

The main downside of hosting at your house includes one heck of a mess to clean up when it is over. (Tip Number One—Hire a cleaning service for the day *after* the party. Doing it the day before is silly because no one can see the dirt once more than five people are in the house, anyway! Just hit it with some Windex and some Fantastik. Put away your laundry, and you're all set!)

Another downside to having it at your place is it may limit the number of people you can invite. If you have pets, kids, or a spouse who isn't too into it, it may be a bother to get them out for the evening or even a few hours. You may not have room to invite everyone who would like to come. Your home may be in an inaccessible location, or far from the place most of the guests will be coming from (which drastically reduces attendance!).

You might not want to have the shower at your house for any of these reasons, and they are all good things to think of when you are deciding on the location. Location is often the biggest expense for an outside shower, so if you're on a shoestring, either do it at your house or get a collaborator with more square footage to help you throw it. One word of caution,

though. Whoever's house it is at is the person who will be blamed or thanked for throwing the shower, no matter what the invitations say!

Five Reasons to Have It at Your House

1. It's cheaper.
2. It's easier to prepare for.
3. You won't have to schlep any stuff.
4. You can decorate and cook in advance.
5. It's cheaper.

Five Reasons *Not* to Have It at Your House

1. The mess people make.
2. The mess you already made and would have to clean first.
3. Getting rid of your pets, kids, or significant other for a few hours.
4. Space considerations.
5. The inconvenience of your location.

How to Find a Good Spot to Rent

Renting a location is a perfect option if (a) your house is too small or inconvenient; (b) you can afford to pay someone else to handle all the crazy details; (c) you just don't want to handle all the crazy details; or (d) you simply prefer it this way.

Whatever your reasons, you will want to choose a rental space that has all the features you will require for your event. The place should be conveniently located, have plenty of good lighting in the parking lot, and meet the criteria of your theme and your general expectations. You will probably need to call and go look at several places before you find the right one for you. Look under "Rental" or "Hotels" in the Yellow Pages.

Some places will give you access to their kitchen and some will connect you with their caterer. Most will *NOT* allow you to bring in your own food or cooking supplies, so make sure you know precisely what you'll need before you deposit any money.

Once you've decided on a place, ask the manager to set aside the date in writing, preferably in the form of a contract. Basically, the contract should state the following things:

1. The date of the event
2. How long you will have the space for
3. What is included
4. Which room (by name) it is that you will be renting
5. How much you must pay
6. How much you must put down to hold the room
7. When the balance is due
8. What happens if you have to cancel

What happens if you have to cancel is especially important. You want to be sure that if your bride calls off her wedding, you can get most of your money back. Most places will let you have some or all of it back up until a month before the event, and then the amount goes down.

Sometimes, an unscrupulous place will let you book a certain room, and then at the last minute, they will try to push you into another room that you didn't want. That's why you must get the name of the room in writing. Be a good businesswoman about this rental contract, and you'll be fine.

It's impossible for me to give you good estimates on how much a rental space will cost, because the factors that determine cost are region, space, demand, and condition.

Checklist of Things to Take If You're Hosting the Shower at a Rented Location

- ❐ Masking tape
- ❐ Scissors
- ❐ A box knife or a pocketknife
- ❐ Pushpins or paneling nails (take a bunch)
- ❐ Duct tape
- ❐ Toothpicks (for rolling the tips of paper tablecloths before you nail them down so they don't blow off in the breeze, and myriad other purposes)
- ❐ Scotch tape
- ❐ A spool of coated wire with snips or some twist-tie wire (like from the produce department)
- ❐ A whisk broom and dustpan
- ❐ A roll of paper towels
- ❐ A bar of soap (maybe?)
- ❐ Bandages
- ❐ Aspirin
- ❐ Tampons
- ❐ Large paper clips (can be opened to form hooks for hanging things from the ceiling in rooms with ceiling tiles)
- ❐ Roll of toilet paper (maybe?)
- ❐ A cooler?
- ❐ Large trash bags
- ❐ Your makeup kit (because you will probably get sweaty setting up)
- ❐ Instant glue (in case someone breaks a nail, or more importantly, in case you have to fix something really quick)
- ❐ Three or four large preprinted signs that say "Debbie's Shower" and have a place you can draw an arrow
- ❐ A big black marker
- ❐ Any decorating items you plan to use

CHAPTER FIVE

Inviting
the Guests

When Should We Have the Shower?

Tradition dictates you have the shower two to four weeks before the wedding. But if your principal guests are from out of town, anytime before the wedding is proper, even a few days before. Think about when her best friend(s) will be in town, and plan accordingly.

Which Day Should We Have the Shower?

Girls-only showers are usually held in the evenings or on weekends, coworker showers during the workday or at the end of one, and coed showers in the evenings or Sunday.

Popular shower options include: Saturday afternoon barbecue, Sunday brunch, evening cocktails, or dinner or dessert during the week.

What Is the Best Time of Day to Have the Shower?

Take into account how far people will have to come, people's work schedules, the bride's own schedule, and other things when planning your time.

Right after work works out well for a coworker party, because everyone is already there. You'd want to go somewhere for dinner if you do that.

For a barbecue, you would typically invite people to come around 4:30 or 5 P.M. and continue on into the evening. For a brunch, you'd probably give a 10 or 10:30 A.M. time and party on through noon. For a shower after church, the time will set itself.

How Long Is a Typical Shower?

An evening dessert-and-coffee girls-only shower would probably last about three hours, but advertise it in the invitations as lasting only two. You'd want to start it late enough so everyone can get through traffic from work, eat dinner, and still make it end early enough so everyone can get up the next day for work.

If you are planning a weekend shower, especially a coed one, the sky's the limit on time. Figure about five hours. Advertise four in your invitations.

If you're trying to answer this question for catering/ room-rental purposes, use three hours as a rule of thumb. Two hours is how long it will officially last, and the third hour will be for happy hangers-on to chat with your bride and straggle out.

Who Should I Invite?

Luckily, your bride probably can give you a really good answer to this question. Your job is just to figure out how many people you want at the shower and tell her.

Obviously, if you're hosting a coworkers-only shower, and you're a coworker, this is a no-brainer and you don't even need to tell the bride. Similarly for church, where you would probably know all her friends.

Some people will tell you you can invite only people who are also invited to the wedding, and some people don't think that matters. It truly doesn't matter if the people who will be at the shower won't be at the wedding for some good reason anyway. Like, if she's getting married in Missouri and you and your local friends of hers all live in Phoenix. Lots of people won't be able to make

Bridal Shower Guests

mimi
grammy K.
Debbie
Betsy
Sarah
Skyler
Kelley
Helen
Janet
Ruth
gina
ann
Laureen
amy
aunt Judy
Kate
Theresa
aunt Reba
Samantha
nicole
Heather
carolyn
Emma

it anyway, so invite whomever you choose.

If she's having a small wedding, a remarriage, or a wedding far away from where she lives or you live, invite anyone you want, as long as she likes the person and you don't invite any of her ex-boyfriends.

Showers held at a club, office, or church, of course, would include acquaintances or colleagues who might not be invited to the wedding.

Frankly, I think people will make their own choices about whether or not they want to attend the shower. If they are upset about not being invited to the wedding and boycott the shower because of it, so much the better. Weddings are supposed to be happy times, so why not invite everyone who cares about the bride and see who shows up with an RSVP?

Remember, the bride is the one who has the final say on whom you invite, unless you have decided on a surprise shower (see the section on surprise showers in Chapter 2). Show her the guest list.

Do I Need to Invite Her Family to the Shower?

If you are not a family friend, and this is not the only shower, or this is just for coworkers or other people who are not expected to know the family, you probably don't. Ask your bride if there will be another shower her mom and other relatives will be attending. If there is, you need not worry about inviting them. If yours is the only shower, or if you personally are friends with the family, then certainly invite them.

Think about this fact before you decide the theme for your shower! You might be pretty embarrassed to invite her grandma to a lingerie wedding shower, and imagine how your bride would feel!

However, if you invite her family, it is absolutely mandatory that you also invite the womenfolk from her groom's family, too!

Can Children Come to the Shower?

Heck, no! If your bride-to-be is a single mom right now, you could theoretically have the shower at Chuck E. Cheese, a particularly loud, blaring, glaring pizza restaurant/ indoor amusement park that little kids adore and most parents loathe), although I doubt that would go over big with most of the other women!

But you can sure have kids show up if the bride is (a) a mom already or (b) about to be a mom. Otherwise, skip the kids.

How about Guys?

Sure, guys can come. This is often fun for the groom, who might not be as involved in the whirl of prewedding celebrations as the bride. (Of course, he could be happy about this, you might want to ask him.) If you invite men, make sure you invite a few single guys if you have a few single girls coming, unless the whole thing is couples. (Try to find *cute* single guys—ask the groom for help!) Many a match began with meeting at someone else's wedding or related festivities. If your shower includes men, it's best to have it in the evening or on Sunday. The shower category or theme, however, should be something of interest to the bride and the groom if he's going to be there. Try something like a Bottle and Bar shower (where every gift has to be in one of those containers or forms); workshop, garden, or barbecue showers are all appropriate.

How Many People Should I Invite?

A typical at-home shower has about fifteen guests, plus the bride and you. Think about the location and time of day you'll be having it if you want to change from these norms.

In reality, if you invite twenty people, fifteen will probably show up, despite RSVPs assuring you everyone will be there. A rule of thumb I always use is plan food for 20 percent more people than I invited, and plan seating for 20 percent less. Something always happens at the last minute.

When Do I Send the Invitations?

Mail the invitations so they arrive no less than two weeks before your shower's date. Figure it takes seven days for an invitation mailed first class to get across the country, four days for a neighboring state, and two days for a local address.

If you are inviting people from out of town to the shower, remember that airline reservations are much, much cheaper if they are made at least thirty days in advance, so work that into your schedule. I always find that six weeks' notice seems to cover all the bases.

Before you mail the invitations, make sure the bride can make it, and if you are using an outside facility, that you have confirmed your reservation with a deposit.

I Want to Do Something Unique with the Invitations. Got Any Ideas?

If you're the least bit creative, you might find it great fun to make the invitations yourself. You can buy lovely printed invitations or you can make them out of construction paper. You can laser-print them on paper you decorated or bought. Nobody said you have to buy the preprinted fill-in-the-blank kind!

If the shower will be at work, you can make a three-dimensional invitation, like a paper flower on a stem, that you can just set on people's desks. If you have to mail them, as you will in most cases, you'll need to make sure that your art project will fit into standard-sized envelopes!

For a Hawaiian shower I once threw, I bought green, yellow, and red tissue paper. I pressed it flat and cut out flower shapes. Then I scored the petals so they had depth, stapled them, and covered the staple with a dollop of red paint and glue I mixed together. I sprinkled it with gold glitter and attached it to a sheet of ordinary computer paper that had the actual invitation information on it.

Ideas for cute invitations could come to you from the theme of your shower. I've included some suggestions in the themes themselves. People will be amused and delighted by your cleverness because so few adults take the time to personalize anything anymore. No matter how common or sophisticated your intended party, handmade invitations can make a huge impression and even attract people to your event.

Skim back through the themes to see some invitation ideas. One from a theme other than the one you've chosen might spark a clever idea.

What Do I Include with the Invitations?

If you want to make your own life easier, you will definitely not forget to include these things with the invitation:

- Date, time, and length of the shower

- Whom guests may bring (kids, dogs, spouses or mates?)

- The name and location of the bridal registry

- The name of the bride and correct spelling of her groom's name

- A map to your house/the location (see the section "How Do I Make Sure Everyone Gets to My House?" in this chapter—and follow the directions given exactly!)

- A description of the theme, if appropriate

- Appropriate gift selections for your theme

- An assigned type of dish if you are having a potluck (e.g., please bring a green salad that can serve ten people)

- If you are serving a meal

- What to wear, if necessary (e.g., everyone wears the wedding colors, or semiformal, or swimsuits and jeans)

- RSVP information—MANDATORY if you are serving a meal or having one catered

- A deadline to respond to the RSVP

How Do I Make Sure They All Get to My House?

People tend to understand directions in one of three ways. You should cover all three by including the following with your invitation: a small map (indicating north) that gives the route to your guests, a list of visual clues, and a set of written instructions, such as:

If you are coming South on the 405, take Elliott exit. Go right. Pass the 76 station (on your right) to the next light, Waldorf Street. Go left 2 blocks, past the park.

If you are coming North on the 405, take Elliot exit. Go left . . .

Use the visual cues (unless it will be pitch dark when the shower takes place and no one will <u>see</u> your visual cues) as well as written directions and an actual little map. Have someone else draw it if you're not good at it.

This is really important because people tend to get flustered when they get lost, and it will not put them in the best mood for your shower. Your guests will be totally grateful for this bit of extra help, cued to the way they understand directions best. Further, you can double check it for accuracy and save yourself answering two or three phone calls from hopelessly lost guests frantic to get there in time on the day of the party!

I Want to Make Sure All Her Best Friends Show Up. Any Ideas?

Getting the people most important to the bride to the shower is something you must think about when you set the date and time. Although surely everyone will try to rearrange their schedule to accommodate whatever time you select, if one or more of her closest friends will be out of town when you have decided to hold the shower, it's going to be sad. The easiest way to prevent this from happening is to decide who these people are and call them in advance—before you decide on a definite date! Make sure it works for them before you invite everyone else.

How Do I Track the RSVPs?

Being organized is the secret of successful events. I've catered dozens of parties of all sorts, and I guarantee, being organized is the most critical part of a flawless event at which you can have fun, too. Figuring out who will be there is very important.

First, know that whatever responses you get, attendance will fluctuate by about 20 percent on the actual day. Someone will get sick, but someone else will probably decide they can make it after all. Just accept it.

Here's how to handle your RSVPs. First, generate a list of those you invited. If you created the labels for the envelopes on a computer, this is easy. Give yourself a sheet of paper with six columns. (See page 81 for a sample. Heck, photocopy it and use it if you want!) When good people call by your deadline to RSVP, make a check in the Coming or Not Coming column and GET THEIR PHONE NUMBERS right then. Call those who don't respond by the morning after your deadline. Get their numbers from the bride if you don't already have them. Call them twice. If they still don't respond, not only are they socially inept, they are highly unlikely to show up, so you can count them out. Don't waste any brain space on this.

When you call to follow up on an RSVP, here's what to say:

"Hi, I'm Janet Harding. I'm hosting Elaine Goldman's wedding shower. Did you get the invitation?"

They answer, "Oh yeah! I meant to call you!"

You say, "I am wondering if you'll be able to make it. I'm confirming the food now, and I want to be able to count on you."

They answer. It's over.

Or, if you don't get them, leave a message like this:

"Hi, I'm Janet Harding. I'm hosting Elaine Goldman's wedding shower. I sent you an invitation but I haven't heard back from you. I'm calling to follow up. Can you please call me back tonight before 11 P.M. at 310-555-1212? Thanks so much! I know it's really important to Elaine that you be invited, and I'm trying to confirm the catering arrangements."

See how easy this is? If you REALLY hate this idea, get one of the women who said they want to help you with the shower to do it for you. Just make sure they DO it.

OK, now if they don't follow up within a day or two of your message/conversation with a commitment, then call again three days after your first calls. ANYONE who doesn't respond is either out of town, sick, or not interested (or just rude).

You're planning on a 20 percent change ratio anyway, but using this foolproof, proven method, you're bound to get most of your answers.

RSVP Chart

Use *this chart to help you determine exactly who will be attending your party.*

NAME	PHONE #	COMING	NOT COMING	CALL 1	CALL 2
1.					
2.					
3.					
4.					
5.					
6.					
7.					
8.					
9.					
10.					
11.					
12.					
13.					
14.					
15.					

RSVP Chart

NAME	PHONE #	COMING	NOT COMING	CALL 1	CALL 2
16.					
17.					
18.					
19.					
20.					
21.					
22.					
23.					
24.					
25.					
26.					
27.					
28.					
29.					
30.					

CHAPTER SIX

Ringing the Dinner Bell

What Do I Feed These People?

If your guests will be there between 8 and 10 A.M., you'd better serve breakfast. If they're there between noon and 1, plan to serve them lunch (a cold cuts buffet is fine). If they are there after work, and it's for more than drinks, plan on feeding them dinner. If it's after the "American dinner hour" (which means after 6:30 P.M.), they will likely all have already eaten and only expect cake and beverages. Any other time, snacks are totally appropriate, and cake is required.

Planning Your Menu

If you are hosting a shower for a friend who is kosher, vegetarian, vegan, or some other religious and/or dietetic discipline, it would be thoughtful of you to be considerate. Ask the bride, for instance, if she cares if you serve shrimp to the nonkosher guests, or red meat to the nonvegetarians. If a preponderance of your guests are of one dietetic persuasion or another, you would be wise to get some recipes from someone so you can cater it to everyone's liking.

Designing the Menu

Take your time designing the menu for the shower. If you are planning to serve something more than cake and cookies, you will need to plan out what you want so that your meal not only looks balanced but elegant, too. Your goal is to create the most wonderful dishes, probably with a minimum of expense. Planning ahead is what will make that happen.

Certain foods are associated with certain activities—peanuts and hot dogs at ball games, for instance. Your first step is to think about what foods mean something to you—which ones would fit in best with the theme of the party you are planning? If you are having a Hawaiian party, you would necessarily choose foods that have a Polynesian flair—things like sweet-and-sour meatballs with pineapple chunks, fruit punch, maybe pineapple upside-down cake.

Similarly, if the party is themed on a country or ethnic group, the food would probably be comfortably representative of that region.

The easiest way to serve food for more than six guests is a buffet. I will assume you are planning to serve whatever you cook buffet style if you are reading this section. (Specific notes for formal, sit-down dinners come later, as well as a brief section on barbecues.) Once you have determined which type of cuisine to feed your guests, you are ready to consider the three most important items in buffet service:

Appearance, flavor, and variety

If you are having the event catered, you will have X dollars to feed X people, and that's it. This will greatly limit the amount you can spend. Further, most places will *not* allow you to supplement their in-house catering department with things you bring in from the outside.

If you are not hiring a caterer, then you will most likely be doing it yourself with some help from your friends. You need to take control of the menu right from the start. If you are planning on having it potluck, you will need to be extremely specific in the invitations in requesting what it is you want your guests to bring. (See "What Do I Include with the Invitations?" on page 78.) You will need to determine precisely what you want and then be as specific as possible with your guests. You can even go so far as to send recipe cards and have guests make and bring the item on them. (This is not usually the way to win a popularity contest, however!)

The easiest way to get others to help you and not screw up your party's meal is to assign everyone something and give everything a backup. In other words, you tell Jill to bring a green salad and Tonya to bring a green salad, too. The worst that can happen is you end up with two green salads.

Otherwise, you can simply do it yourself.

Planning for Variety on Your Buffet Table

Focus on "eye appeal" when you plan any party menu. Think of how the food will actually look when it is sitting on the buffet table or on someone's plate when you are choosing what you want to serve. You will definitely want an interesting variety of colors, textures, flavors, and sizes.

Choose no more than five major dishes for a buffet. That keeps everything much simpler and creates a more elegant appearance. Since you will likely not be hiring anyone to serve the guests as they pass through the line, having more of fewer dishes also motivates people to move through the line faster because they have fewer items to sample.

For a real meal, your dishes would most likely include the following:

- ✿ One hot meat dish

- ✿ One hot fish or poultry dish

- ✿ A starch, ranging from pasta salad, rice, potatoes, or rolls

- ✿ A green salad

- ✿ Some sort of vegetable dish, either hot or cold

- ✿ And for dessert, the cake, possibly with ice cream and/or a fruit salad.

If a budget has you constricted so that you are planning the party at a nonmeal time, or if you simply want to keep it very simple, why not try something like the following hors d'oeuvres menu:

- Crackers or interesting bread

- One or two kinds of cheese (perhaps Brie and Colby)

- An interesting fruit platter or fruit salad

- A vegetable item (even as simple as carrot sticks and dip)

- Some nuts or salty snack food like pretzels

- The cake

How Much Do I Need to Feed Each of Them? How Much Food Does a Typical Woman Eat?

The typical American female eats precisely 7.0287 ounces of food at a wedding shower, not counting the obligatory piece of cake. OK, I made that up. Figure 1 1/3 servings per woman. In my own mother's words, "It's better to have too much than to send your guests home hungry." The only time Mama is wrong is if you are hiring a caterer and it's costing you big bucks to be wrong. (But since you have carefully gotten your RSVPs back, you know precisely how many people to plan for.)

If you figure a serving is one hamburger, one chicken breast, one cup of pasta with sauce, and so on, and you plan 1 1/3 servings per person, you will hit it just about perfect. I always consider any dinner a success if I have at least two servings left when the dishes return to the kitchen. (If there were only one serving, you'd figure someone was too polite to eat the last of it but was still hungry.)

If you are serving cold cuts or a buffet, you'd want to roughly calculate 3 ounces of meat per person and 1½ servings of bread.

If you are serving just canapés and deli plates with carrot sticks and other finger food, you can probably figure on about 1 1/2 cups of food, loosely chopped, per person. That will give you a bit extra, but it's easy to figure. For instance, if you can fit one cut up taquito, a few nuts, three carrot sticks, and two cherry tomatoes into 1 1/2 cups, you've got it about right. (P.S.—When serving finger foods, use six-inch plates, not the big ones, which encourage waste and screw up your planning per person.) People eat less in the summer and at certain times of day. If you've ever been to a buffet, you may have noticed that the cheap, bulky items are always put first, before the meats and expensive stuff. You can set up your line the same way—put the pasta and green and fruit salads at the beginning of the line and the meats later.

People, especially women, eat less in public than they might at home, so you can count on that, too. Nobody's likely to waddle away from your buffet with two full plates of chow.

For the cake, plan on everyone taking one piece and there still being a few slices left over.

For beverages, a general rule of thumb is two cups of liquids per person per hour. If we're talking alcohol, it changes, of course, depending on the potency. Two beers in an hour may be reasonable, but so would three ounces of a strong liqueur.

The official guidelines in several catering books, party planning books, and cookbooks say basically this:

> Hors d'oeuvres: 3–4 per person per hour
> Meat, poultry, and fish: About 3 oz. per person
> Fruit salad: 4–6 oz. per person
> All other kinds of salad: About 2 oz. per person
> Breads, rolls, etc.: 1–1½ servings per person (make sure you slice breads in advance).
> Dessert: One slice of cake per person

Can I Do This Potluck?

Dreams come true! Everyone brings something and you don't have to worry! But don't take the huge risk of allowing people to choose for themselves what they want to bring. No! On the invitations, you must write clearly, "Please bring a green salad that will serve 10 people" or "Please bring 2 quarts of pineapple juice" or you will end up with twenty-five bags of chips!

How Can I Feed These People Cheaply and Still Make It Look Nice?

In California, we have a wonderful place called "Smart&Final." This is a place where the restaurants go to get their bulk supplies. Check your Yellow Pages under "Restaurant Supplies." If that doesn't work, see if you can find a Price Club or a Costco or one of their many competitors nearby. It may well be worth the lack of service, long lines, and the price of a membership card to shop for the party there.

Buy the things you don't like to make. If you can shape hamburger patties but wouldn't get a kick out of making your own BBQ sauce, buy the sauce and save the money by buying the meat in bulk.

When you write your shopping list, write down the quantities you need of each item by using the provided measurements as rules of thumb. When you shop, decide where to cut corners to save yourself time. In general, buy higher-quality cheeses and meats and breads, and you can buy the less-expensive condiments and peripheral stuff.

I Don't Have Much Time to Cook the Day of the Party. Now What?

If you are running out of time, or know you will be rushed the day of the party, buy some eternal favorites like potato chips and pretzels and dump them into pretty bowls. People love snack foods. And your job does not include serving things that would fit nicely onto the food pyramid. This is a party, you can be liberal. It's OK to choose things that are prepackaged.

If you're really short on time and money, for a nice luncheon buffet, follow this 10-Step "You're-an-Amazing-Hostess" Shopping Plan

1. Go to your local grocery store a few days early and see if they can put together a few platters of cut-up vegetables (carrots, celery, jicama, broccoli, etc.) with some sort of dip if the dip is included. (If it's extra, they have great ones in the dairy case.) Pick up the platters on the day of the party. Or buy the veggies loose.

2. If you have fifteen women coming, go buy yourself two or three bags of chips—corn chips, Doritos, potato chips, whatever. Get the yummy kind.

3. Buy a block of Velveeta cheese, a can of diced stewed tomatoes with onions, and two cans of refried beans.

4. Buy three ounces of different kinds of cold cuts for each room. (That's forty-five ounces for fifteen women, which is about three pounds.)

5. Buy some presliced cheese or get the deli guy to slice it for you.

6. Buy twenty-two different kinds of sandwich rolls, a jar of interesting mustard, and some basic mayo and American mustard.

7. Buy a head of Romaine lettuce, a bunch of parsley, an orange, and a lemon.

8. Go pick up the cake in the bakery department that you ordered two weeks ago.

9. Buy two cans of pineapple juice, two quarts of 7-Up, one can of Hawaiian punch.

10. Go home and put it all together as follows:

The Do-It-Yourself 12-Step Shower Catering Plan

Step 1: Wash the vegetables if you are assembling the platters yourself.

Step 2: Get out a big platter or tray and two or three baskets. If you don't have a tray or platter, wrap aluminum foil around a big piece of wood or the side of a cardboard box.

Step 3: Chop up the Velveeta into chunks, dump in the beans and tomatoes, and microwave for a few minutes until you can stir it smooth. Set it aside.

Step 4: Take the matching paper napkins for the party and line the baskets with them.

Step 5: Slap the washed, dried romaine lettuce along the tray or platter, with the dark green part along the edges and the bottom parts all in the center.

Step 6: Lay the meats and cheeses in an attractive pattern on the platter. I'd probably alternate them. Garnish with parsley, two orange slices, and two lemon slices. Put on table.

Step 7: Dump the chips into a lined basket, and arrange the bread in the other one or two.

Step 8: Put the Velveeta dip into a serving bowl. Stick a sprig of parsley into it and a lemon wedge. (It's good lukewarm, so don't freak out if it cools down!)

Step 9: With a rubber spatula, spoon the condiments into small glass bowls. Garnish with parsley.

Step 10: Unwrap the vegetable platters and put them on the table.

Step 11: In a big punch bowl, mix half of the beverage ingredients you bought. Add the floating ice ring and all the leftover citrus slices you can float on top.

Step 12: Put the cake and whatever other table decorations you want to use in a spot of honor on the table. Arrange the paper goods and relax! You've just catered it yourself!

Total estimated time (not including shopping or preordering): 1½ hours.

What Can I Prepare in Advance?

The day before, you can cut up the crudités (cold vegetables like carrots and celery) and put them, wrapped in a damp paper towel, in a plastic bag, or float them in a jar of cold water in the fridge.

You can do any baking that will be necessary for the party. If you are making the cake yourself, definitely bake it the day before. Then, after it cools, brush off the crumbs with a pastry brush and slip it into a plastic bag. Store it in the freezer until three hours before the party. That way, it will be very easy to decorate.

You can wash and store any garnishes you intend to use—like lettuce, parsley, and so forth. You can make the rice and even the pasta if you add a little oil to keep it moist. Pasta salads should be made the day before to give the flavors time to meld.

Marinate your meat now. Chop vegetables to be grilled and seal them in plastic.

What Should I Not Prepare in Advance?

Don't try to make in advance anything made with apples or bananas, like a fruit salad. (In fact, up to an hour before the guests get there, if you have to use an apple or banana for anything, dip the pieces in a solution of one cup of water and the juice of half a lemon.)

Do not slice any baked goods until a few hours before the party.

Unless you and your freezer understand each other extremely well, you should not attempt to create any frozen desserts, like an ice cream pie or whipped cream for strawberry shortcake, prior to the event. The temperature is almost never right when you go to serve it.

Don't mix the punch or add ice to anything until moments before the guests arrive.

Don't get all mayonnaise-d out before the shower and end up giving people salmonella. Keep anything with mayo in the fridge until the last minute.

How Do I Make a Shower Cake Easily and Fast?

It's a lot of fun to make and decorate your own cake, and cheaper, too. If easy is called for, get a cake mix in chocolate or vanilla. If you get chocolate, add ½ cup of chocolate chips to the mix right before you pour it into the pan. If you use vanilla, throw in 1 cup of frozen raspberries or raisins or diced peaches.

For the filling, try pudding or jam instead of the frosting that you can buy premade. I always make my own frosting, but if you don't want to, those little tubs of it work great. Figure it will take two of them to neatly cover a nine-inch layer cake.

Freeze the cake when it's cooled from the oven (the day before the shower). Then, while it's still frozen, brush off any crumbs with a pastry brush. Frost it while it's thawing. (It takes about three hours to thaw if it's not assembled. Frost it cold, especially if it's hot in your house!) Smear frosting on with the flat side of a table knife. Work from the top down—dump lots of frosting on the top and smooth it over the edges. Once it's over the edges, come around with the flat side of the knife again to make it perfect.

With a few metal spatulas, lift the cake onto a clean plate for final decorating. (That's how I do it—my cake-decorating teacher had much more fancy ideas about using waxed paper rings before you ice it.)

If you're adventurous in the kitchen, you probably already know how to make scallops and loops around the edges with a bag of icing. If you don't, just smooth out the icing as best you can. Sprinkle it with something interesting, like candy hearts (very appropriate) or colored candy beads. Be creative!

 What You'll Need to Make a Shower Cake

1 box of cake mix
2 tubs of frosting (get white frosting and some food coloring if they don't have frosting in the color you want)
2 layer pans for cakes
About ½ cup of flour, for flouring the pans
A bit of butter or some no-stick cooking spray
A butter knife
A serving plate
Sprinkles, chocolate kisses, or colored candies
A tube of decorating gel
A plastic ornament tied to the shower's theme

How Do I Buy a Shower Cake?

Call four local bakeries, including the one at your local grocery store, to find one who promises you the best shower cake. Drop by to look at their pictures of cakes they've made. Taste something they've baked. If it has that weird lard aftertaste, skip them.

When you find a design you like and a price that fits your budget, order the cake. Expect to put down 50 percent of the final price. Some places will deliver it to your shower location—wouldn't that be nice? Imagine driving with the cake in your car!

You should order the cake at least two weeks in advance, and you should know when you order it how many people you will want it to serve. A basic round layer cake serves eight to ten people. An 11"×9"×2" sheet cake (the proper term for flat cakes) will service fifteen people fairly easily. Don't let the baker talk you into ordering too much cake!

Is Alcohol Appropriate? Is It Required?

Serving alcohol is never required, but it is mandatory that you provide nonalcoholic beverages if you are serving liquor. It's also a nice touch to have a pitcher of water with a floating lemon slice in it on the table. But as for alcohol, unless you'd like to spend the big bucks, it's far easier to spike the punch than to provide beer or wine or champagne for the whole crew.

Although most wedding showers feature nonalcoholic beverages, you might choose to add some alcoholic ones to your party. The only rule about alcohol at parties is that the hostess must watch for overconsumption and take appropriate measures to avert disaster.

Many cookbooks offer splendid recipes for alcoholic punches. For a party of all women, you would likely choose a light, fruity alcoholic punch.

Generally, the amounts you should plan on are as follows:

- 1 bottle of wine = 6–8 filled glasses

- 1 quart of hard liquor = 20 1½-oz. drinks

- 1 20-oz. bottle of champagne = 8 glasses

- ½ keg of beer = 260 8-oz. glasses

- 2 gallons of punch = 64 4-oz. punch cups

Fish House Punch

1 bottle	peach brandy
1 bottle	light rum
2 bottles	dry white wine
1 quart	club soda or
	sparkling water
1½ cups	lemon juice
½ cup	fine sugar

Dissolve sugar in lemon juice and brandy. Add rum and wine. Stir. Refrigerate. Pour into a punch bowl over ice. Add club soda just before serving. Approximately 25 servings.

Claret Cup

2 bottles	dry red wine
½ cup	blackberry brandy
½ cup	Triple Sec
½ cup	lemon juice
1 cup	orange juice
2 Tbs.	grenadine
	sliced fruit

Combine ingredients and pour into a punch bowl over ice. Garnish with fruit. Approximately 15 servings.

Cape Cod Punch

3 cups	vodka
2 quarts	cranberry juice
1 quart	orange juice
½ cup	lemon juice
½ cup	fine sugar
1 quart	mineral water

Dissolve sugar in juices in a large bowl. Add vodka. Stir well. Pour over ice into a punch bowl. Add water before serving. Approximately 30 servings.

Bishop's Punch

2 bottles	sweet red wine
¼ cup	cognac
4	oranges studded
	with cloves
¼ tsp.	cinnamon
¼ tsp.	nutmeg

Bake oranges on a cookie sheet in a 400 degree oven for 30 minutes or until soft. Heat liquors and spices, but do not boil. Place the oranges in a punch bowl. Add wine and cognac. Approximately 12 servings.

Nonalcoholic Drinks

As more and more people become health conscious, fewer and fewer drink alcohol. Either way, a good hostess always provides at least some nonalcoholic drinks. The obvious basics are coffee, hot and/or iced tea, and cool water, preferably with a few floating lemon wedges. Other beverages to consider include:

- Lemonade
- Fruit punch
- Sparkling apple juice
- Bottled water
- Soft drinks
- Fruit juice
- Vegetable juice

You'd probably serve any of the above with a few lemon or lime wedges available, or set a punch bowl filled with cans or bottles and ice on the table.

Of course, the traditional drink at wedding showers is fruit punch, usually with sherbet floating on top. The recipe follows:

Basic Nonalcoholic Punch

2 quarts of lemon-lime soda
1 half-gallon of lemon-lime-orange sherbet
2 quarts of pineapple juice
1 quart of pink grapefruit juice

Mix half now, and half halfway through the party.

What about Catering the Shower?

Catering is a wonderful idea but very expensive. If you want someone to cater your party in your home, be prepared to pay a premium. If you want to have it at an establishment that offers catering, talk to the catering manager there. Be advised that few places that offer catering will allow you to bring in food from the outside, so check first before you decide to cut corners and bring in a cake from the local bakery instead of theirs.

If you are hiring a catering company to come to your house, speak to several of them before you make up your mind. Try to get recommendations of good caterers from friends. Also, read the tips for catering the party yourself, earlier in this chapter. People aren't coming because you are a gourmet, they're coming because they love the bride.

An average catered meal will run you between $17–$32 per person, rule of thumb. The nice thing: They do the dishes!

5 Steps to a Flawless Catered Event

Step 1: If you are using a rented space, confirm that they allow outside caterers, if there are kitchen facilities at the site and if you may use them, who is responsible if something breaks, what they provide, and so forth. They may have their own or preferred caterers.

Step 2: Look for a caterer with credentials! Meet four of them at least. Get someone certified by the state you live in as a real, true caterer. Find them through referral or recommendation. Call a few people they use as referrals and actually find out how they liked the service and the food!

Step 3: Get it in writing! Find out what the cancellation terms are; how much you have to deposit and when; how many people they will serve and for what price; what food exactly they will serve; if they will provide utensils, plates, etc. Know precisely what you are getting for what you are paying. Know what happens if they cancel or screw up, or if your bride breaks her engagement and you cancel the party. Lots of people have lost money on nonrefundable deposits this way.

Step 4: Do you like and trust the caterer? Have you met several of them? Do they make you feel pressured, like they are cramming things down your throat? Trust your instincts! Have you sampled their food? How many servers will show up at the event? You need at least two to run a banquet table, at least one bartender/drinks person and two kitchen staff if you're having a buffet meal.

Step 5: Who is going to be in charge on the shower day? Will the person you are meeting actually show up? What will they do? What will be required of you, specifically? Get everything in writing. Let me repeat that: Get everything in writing. OK, for the last time, *Get everything in writing!* (You've been warned.)

Can I Cater Just Part of It?

Absolutely! There's no rule here! Your local deli would love to prepare some cold meat platters, hot dishes, or crudités! This is a great way to save time. Just make sure you confirm the contents of the platter and when you will pick it up. I suggest you pick it up yourself the morning of the shower, because sending someone else might mean the deli sends them home with vegetables when you were expecting a meat tray. The prices for these trays vary widely, but they sure help out in a pinch!

Of course, if you have the least bit of artistic flair, you can create great-looking trays much cheaper yourself. Buy some big disposable platters, some precut meats, some radishes and lettuce for garnishes. At $5.99 per pound for cold cuts, you'd still be ahead of the game doing it yourself and rolling and arranging each piece of meat.

CHAPTER SEVEN

Decorating Your Party:

All about Room Decorations

*D*ecorating for the party is so much fun! Planning how you will decorate and make the environment interesting is exciting. You can create an ambience to match your theme using items appropriate to your theme, but there are some basics to decorating for every party: choosing the right colors, using flowers and the festive arrangement of food, using traditional decorations like paper goods and balloons.

It's easy to make all these things work together if you follow the simple ideas in this book. You're sure to have lots of ideas of your own to add. You can get everything to match, or you can make vibrant contrasts. Different colors stimulate people in different ways, so think about that when you are planning your shower. You may want to match the wedding colors, or you may want to do something totally different. It's your choice!

Party Goods

Just about the easiest way to stylize a party, if not the least expensive, is to buy all the matching paper goods at once—before you even send out the invitations. Trot down to Michael's, Hallmark, or even Wal-Mart, and you'll find a whole section of matching paper goods. Or look under "Party" in your Yellow Pages, especially if you live near a big city.

Items you can find that will match your chosen colors, theme, or the wedding colors can include:

Invitations
Paper plates
Paper cups
Plastic flatware
Napkins
Streamers

Japanese lanterns
Glitter and sequins
Balloons
Piñatas
Swizzle sticks
Decorated toothpicks
Decorated straws
Curling ribbon
Fabric ribbon
Silk flowers
Crafter's spray paint
Place cards
Tablecloths
Precut veil (for making sachets or party favors)
Rolls of veil material
Scalloped veil material
At most of these party places, you will find myriad
    plastic thingamabobs for tying to ribbons, putting on
    cakes, adding to invitations. Things like little plastic
    champagne glasses, metallic wedding rings, wedding
    cakes, brides and grooms, slippers, you name it!

Choosing Colors

Colors mean different things to different people. For my six-year-old daughter and me, red and yellow always mean McDonald's, for instance. But did you know that the insides of prisons are often painted a pale rosy pink to calm the inmates? Did you know that lavender and pale blue are serene colors, while red and bright green stir things up? A cool, true indigo is thought to stimulate thinking, and purple is considered the most balanced color, representative of advanced spiritual enlightenment. Yellow is perceived as a happy color and black as a sophisticated, chic statement, especially with metallic highlights.

Decorating the Shower Location

Decorating the shower is a really fun part of hosting it. In half an hour, all the fun items you've hoarded turn into a party atmosphere. How great! This section will give you general decorating ideas. If you have already chosen a specific theme, there are likely to be predictable decorations that go with it, or ones that are suggested in the theme description.

Decorating with Paper

There are many types of paper products you can get to decorate your party with. There are large accordion-fold wedding bells—a traditional decoration for wedding showers—streamers, piñatas, Chinese lanterns, luminarias, and many others. I cannot begin to tell you as much as you will learn from a trip to your party supply store. But I certainly can tell you a big secret about paper products: Unless you live in a very dry climate like Arizona in the summer, do not hang them out the day before! They will get limp and perhaps even be ruined, depending on your climate.

There are many ways to hang paper goods without destroying walls. If you have ceiling tiles, use bent-out large paper clips as holders for balloons and paper goods. If you have a regular flat ceiling, you can use flat thumbtacks—they work much better than pushpins, which are often bright, call attention to themselves, and have a smaller head to affix the decoration with. If you have a stucco ceiling, it is much better if you can avoid trying to nail anything directly into the ceiling because you risk losing chunks of stucco. Instead, thumbtack your decorations to the opposite walls, or attach them to drapery rods with masking tape.

In the event that you really don't want to cause any sort of damage to the ceiling, buy some heavy-gauge fishing line at a sporting goods department. Make a tiny knot in one end, poke the end of a thumbtack through the hole, and nail the tacks into the opposing walls, creating a sort of invisible spider's web on the ceiling. With minimal extra support required, it will hold up all your decorations and be easy to remove.

Decorating with Candles

Tapers that match your party colors, along with interesting candleholders, are lovely. Put them in fish bowls, poke them into the cake, place an elegant silver candelabrum in the middle of your table, light a taper in the bathroom to light the way to that room. Candles are always appropriate. Just be sure they won't tip accidentally and ignite a paper tablecloth, that no tipsy guest will burn himself reaching across them for food or drink, or that they will drip on food you want to serve.

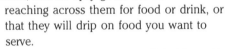

Try decorating your candleholders with flowers, greenery, or even little plastic doodads, but don't use anything flammable, like paper.

Decorating with Balloons

In the minds of most people, balloons mean it's a party! There are two different types of balloons—Mylar (the shiny metallic kind) and rubber (the only kind we had as kids). Mylar are often bigger, more expensive, and always filled with helium. Rubber can be filled with helium, water, or air.

Helium is typical for most parties. Make sure you don't fill the balloons with helium until the last couple of hours before the party, though, because it drains out. Going to the florist's and ordering helium-filled balloons can be expensive, but that's one way to get them easily. Call a week in advance to order them for your big day. The other way to get them is to rent a helium tank from a party store. I even saw a small helium tank (refillable) sold prefilled with some balloons at Target. Helium's combustible, so be careful driving it home, and keep the tank away from heat and flame.

A very, very cool decorating trick is to create a "forest" of balloons on the ceiling, each trailing a long piece of curling ribbon. This would be especially cool if you have high ceilings. Or, you could do short ribbons and tie tiny plastic champagne glasses or other wedding ornaments to them. Make sure you tie several balloons to the special chair you'll create for the bride to sit in.

Decorating the Gift Table

The gift table is where you pile, stow, stack, and dump all the gifts that come for the shower. It is often decorated similarly to the buffet table. If you get fewer gifts than you predicted, simply put a plant or vase of flowers on the table at the last minute, before the bride shows up.

I suggest a "banquet table" about 6 feet in length for this purpose. You would have already picked out your table linens. If you are using a paper tablecloth and you find it does not cover the legs of your table and you want it to, take two plain white tablecloths (paper, plastic, cotton, damask) and slide one down over the front so it covers the legs of the table and touches the floor. Tape it down wherever it comes to on the table with heavy duct tape (the wide silver kind of tape). Cover the tape and whatever overlap with the other white tablecloth.

Do you want to keep your paper-products theme—the pattern on the paper goods you bought for the party? Try the following suggestions.

If you are using a cloth tablecloth underneath: Fold the matching paper tablecloth in half, pretty side out, down the center. Ruck or crinkle or gather it in a nice way. With a ruler, determine the exact middle of your buffet table. Pin it to the table with a large safety pin, using the inside of the pin as a sort of ring. (See illus.) Complete the same on both ends of the table. If you want lovely hanging trails, or if it doesn't reach, add some matching ribbon and pin that to it, too. Don't worry about the pins being ugly. You can wire flowers or bows to them to cover them up.

If you are using a paper tablecloth underneath: Read the instructions above. However, instead of using pins (which would rip your tablecloth), use bits of wire to hold up the decorative paper cloth or ribbons that you poke through the paper tablecloth and tape securely to the flat surface of the table underneath.

The same method works with ribbons or real or fake flower garlands, like maybe fake English Ivy or matching roses. (Look for 6–8-foot-long garlands of silk flowers at the local crafts or floral supply store.)

This material is repeated in the "Buffet Table" sections, but I figured if you weren't serving a meal, you might not see it there and then would not have the information you need.

When You're Ready to Think about Seating Arrangements ...

If you have decided to have a buffet, everyone pretty much expects to fill their plates and find their own place to sit. The only time you really need to worry about everyone sitting at a table is at a barbecue, a formal meal, or when the bride is opening the presents.

Here's how to plan the seating: If you have the shower outdoors, you can rent nifty garden furniture, take any sturdy metal-legged stuff out of your house and put it in the yard, and let people sit on benches, lawn chairs, or whatever. If you are doing it on the grass, DON'T take out any wooden-legged furniture, and test the ground first to make sure it's hard enough to hold someone sitting on it. Some little chair legs will sink right into the dirt and topple your guest!

You can make benches from two really large planters (with something in them, like a big plant!) and two 2" × 4" pieces of lumber. You can rent lawn chairs or make this the perfect occasion to justify buying that patio furniture you have your eye on.

If you are doing it inside, you can also bring in lawn chairs, especially if they aren't too ratty-looking. Usually, the bride sits in the best chair in the house, and it's decorated specially for her. Everyone else is arranged in a sort of horseshoe shape, especially for gift opening.

Set up seating so people can sit in groups of two or more, preferably with little tables to put their stuff on nearby.

Creating the Seat of Honor

Your bride is the guest of honor at your shower, even if the mayor's there. She should have a special chair with optimal views of all the other guests, especially during the gift-opening part of the shower.

One of your wingback chairs will work just fine, as would a captain's chair from your dining room. Decorate it in advance with balloons and lay a streamer across the seat that says "Reserved for Betsy." You could drape it in velvet, plump it up with extra cushions, or spray paint an old chair gold and glue tiny fake jewels from the hobby store to it. You could tie wedding things to its back, like the traditional decorations on the back of the bride and groom's getaway car.

If You're Doing It at Home . . .

A word of caution: If you have fabric-covered sofas, you might want to consider buying a can of Scotchgard and spraying your sofas or chairs a day or two before the event. Nobody is going to want to spill anything, but a lot of people in a small space getting all excited sometimes cause boo-boos. And a big red-wine boo-boo on your white sofa is probably one shower souvenir you don't want!

HELP! I Need Furniture!

Whatever you can think of for this party, somebody somewhere has it for rent, or to buy, cheap. There are hundreds of things you can rent that will help you deal with your decorating. They are usually reasonably priced and you might be able to get the rental company to set them up and take them down for a minimal charge.

Let me tell you this story, though, before you rush out to rent anything you need for the party: I once was planning to have sixty people from my husband's office over for dinner at the same time. I needed two banquet tables for the event. I called the rental company, and they wanted $15 each for the tables, which seemed reasonable at the time. I threw big parties about six times a year, and renting the tables at $15 each ($30 per time), six times per year, would have cost me $180 a year.

Luckily, I went into a hardware store (who would have thought?) and saw the same tables on sale. They were really the identical tables. They were $30 each! I also use them for craft projects and for Thanksgiving and other events. Total investment = $60. So before you rush out to rent something, you might want to check out if it is less expensive to buy it.

The rule of thumb is this: If you will use it more than three times in your life, it's probably cheaper to buy it than rent it. The same is true for lawn furniture. If you have been planning to buy some someday anyway, why not use this as the perfect excuse? Thinking about this makes owning a rental company look like a pretty amazing business, doesn't it?

Cool Stuff You Can Rent for the Party

Canopies	Candles
Tents	Tablecloths
Audio and video equipment	Matching napkins
Tables	Trellises
Chairs	Helium tanks
Dishes	Decorations
Glassware	Silverware
Serving dishes	

Tableware

Like you see in the rental box in this section, you can rent nice stuff from any company. From plates to glasses to serving dishes, the local rental company doubtless has it all. But if you are like me and want to throw it all away and be done with it, I suggest you buy paper or plastic tableware, including napkins, tablecloths, plates, cups, and silverware. My motto is, Why wash it when you can toss it?

All about Party Flowers

Flowers are one of the more fun parts of a shower. You'll want a nice centerpiece for the table, a tiny bouquet for the bathroom, and maybe a nice flat arrangement for your coffee table, if you're doing this at home.

The most obvious choice is to pay somebody to make these bouquets for you. But if you don't want to spend an extra $50 on flowers, take these tips I learned from Tess Kenna at Winslow Floral in Winslow, Arizona. You just might find you have a real knack for it!

First, decide what colors you want. If your party colors match the wedding colors, you can probably figure out flowers that match all by your lonesome. Or stroll through a couple of flower shops. Some better grocery stores sell blooms "by the stem," which is how loose flowers are purchased.

Pick out the kind of flowers you want a few days before the party, but don't buy them until the last minute (that day). You can buy them in the morning for an evening shower if (a) it's cold in your house, (b) you have room in your fridge to store the bouquets/arrangements, or (c) you have no other choice.

Look for flowers without browning edges, and roses that are firm when you squeeze them. Check the base of the flower for tears: This is how florists make roses look younger than they are—they tear off the dying petals from around the outside. You can tell if you look closely. Get the freshest flowers you can. Buy with them a bunch of "leather," those wonderful glossy fern fronds you see in flower arrangements, and some baby's breath (gypsophila) unless you have great, hardy yard flowers at home.

From the florist, ask for a brick of Oasis, which is the green stuff they poke flowers into. (You can also get this at a crafts store.) The florist will probably charge you a buck or so. Ask also for a piece of florist's wire (long, skinny green-coated wire, any size will do fine). If the flowers don't come with a longevity agent, ask for some. This is the powder you mix with the water to make the flowers last longer.

When you get home, put the flowers in the fridge and put the Oasis in a bucket or sink full of water to which you have added the longevity agent. Oasis floats, so weight it with a pot or something. It will fill with water in a while. Give it thirty minutes to soak.

Next, select a pretty, low dish or flower pot or two. Get a sharp knife, your cutting board, and some veined packing tape, duct tape, or florist's tape. Take your wire and use it to cut the Oasis to fit into your pots or dishes. (Cut it like you see them cutting people's necks with wire in gory guy movies.) Stuff little bits of Oasis into the pockets around the sides so it is totally full of green matter—nowhere is there air between the pot and the Oasis. Now tape the Oasis into the pots or dishes with your tape. Two strips in each direction for a pot 6 inches or more in diameter is plenty.

Repeat three times, "This is fun, this is fun."

Take the leather fern and "green the bowl." That means, poke the fronds into the dish or pot so that they leave little spaces, or whorls, where a bloom would fit perfectly, foiled by the dark fern. You will use all the bunch of leather fern on two 6-inch flowerpots. Snip the ends of the fern so the part where the leaf begins is the part resting on the Oasis.

Now, go run around your yard with a pair of pruning shears, picking any wee leafy branches (young lemon or orange branches are lovely) or other interesting plants or flowers you see. Try to avoid garden flowers, except hardy roses, marigolds, hollyhocks, delphiniums, and purple statice, because others will wilt quickly. Stick them at once into a pitcher of water.

Now get your refrigerated flowers out of the fridge. Quickly cut their bases with the paring knife and immediately poke them into the whorls you created with the leather. (The longer you leave a flower's stem exposed to air, the less time it will live. Imagine an air bubble in a diver's bloodstream, and you get the idea. Real florists try to cut it to seconds between snipping the stem and arranging the flower.) Add your yard plants.

Fuss a little if you must, but remember, flower arranging is like geometry—everything in balance. You cannot put six white roses left of center and three right—it will look funny. A simple idea is imagining the bowl cut in half. Put half your blooms on either side, far enough apart so you can enjoy looking at all their petals. Add some filler (either gypsophila from the florist or your yard plants) and you're nearly done.

If you have to pull out the flowers a few times, that's normal. Even professional designers modify their works of art. Mess around with it, have fun, and in a few minutes, voilà! You will have a worthy and attractive centerpiece and a wonderful table spray. Take a few of the extra blooms, slip them into a vase (with treated water in it), and put it in your bathroom.

If you want, tie a balloon or two to small sticks and poke them into the bouquet, too. Stuff in a bow or two, or something else interesting. Maybe you've wired some of the leftover wedding-favor supplies (like little champagne glasses and tin wedding rings) to long skewers and you can poke them in, too.

Congratulations! You're a florist! And you just saved at least $50.

Things you'll need to create great floral arrangements

1. One or two pretty, low bowls or baskets lined with plastic, or perhaps a pretty flowerpot.
2. One big hunk of Oasis (florist's brick), about twice as big as a building brick.
3. A length of florist's wire.
4. A bucket of water.
5. Some sort of floral longevity agent—Sta-Fresh or other brand (available at the florist's).
6. Sturdy tape like duct tape, cut into thin strips, or florist's tape.
7. Six to eight nice blooms per arrangement.
8. A bunch of baby's breath (gypsophila), unless you have some nice flowers in your yard. This serves as filler and offsets the primary blooms.
9. A bundle of "leather," the leafy, glossy fern leaves florists often use.
10. A sharp knife and cutting board.

Food Presentation 101: Decorating Your Buffet Table

Never crowd zillions of foods onto a tray. Ideally, they should not even touch the sides of the tray or platter. Get more platters, or make them from florists' colored foil wrapped around sheets of wood or heavy cardboard.

Select a specific table for the food and a separate one for drinks if you're expecting to serve more than one or two beverage choices. I suggest a banquet table about 6 feet in length for the purposes of the meal you would serve to fifteen women. You can probably rent one for $15, or buy one for $30 at the hardware store or Office or

Home Depot. They store flat, so if you like to entertain, buy it, don't rent it.

You would have already picked out your table linens in the decorating chapter, so let's say this here: If you find your paper tablecloth does not cover the legs of your table and you want it to, take two plain white tablecloths (paper, plastic, cotton, damask) and slide one down over the front so it covers the legs of the table and touches the floor. Tape it down wherever it comes to on the table, with heavy duct tape (the wide silver kind of tape). Cover the tape and whatever overlap with the other white tablecloth.

Do you want to keep your paper products theme—the pattern on the paper goods you bought for the party? Try the following suggestions.

If you are using a cloth tablecloth underneath: Fold the matching paper tablecloth in half, pretty side out, down the center. Ruck or crinkle or gather it in a nice way. With a ruler, determine the exact middle of your buffet table. Pin it to the table with a large safety pin, using the inside of the pin as a sort of ring. (See Illust.) Complete the same on both ends of the table. If you want lovely hanging trails, or if it doesn't reach, add some matching ribbon and pin that to it, too. Don't worry about the pins being ugly. You can wire flowers or bows to them to cover them up.

If you are using a paper tablecloth underneath: Read the instructions above. However, instead of using pins (which would rip your tablecloth), use bits of wire to hold up the decorative paper cloth or ribbons that you poke through the paper tablecloth and tape securely to the flat surface of the table underneath.

The same method works with ribbons or real or fake flower garlands, like maybe fake English Ivy or matching roses. (Look for 6–8-foot-long garlands of silk flowers at the local crafts or floral supply store.)

Decorating the Tabletop

Stack three or four large books, like encyclopedias or dictionaries, slightly off of center on your table. Cover the entire stack with a matching paper tablecloth or a wonderful piece of fabric (velvet? brocade? something that matches the theme of your party?). You can either wrap it around the bottom of the stack, or you can let it flow onto the table surface.

On the top of this, you can put the floral bouquet you made, the shower cake, some interesting centerpiece tied to your theme, whatever. If you put a simple vase of flowers, make it a nice vase and put something a wee bit lower under the vase for variety's sake. (Like a small silver box, a wee plastic wedding couple, a small ceramic bird, etc.)

If you want to put your buffet on different levels, make the stack with the centerpiece highest, and place another dish, maybe a salad in a lovely bowl, on the next tier down.

You may want to run garlands from the centerpiece down to one or more corners of the table. Or you can artfully sprinkle some flower petals or leaves (at the last minute), or some glitter or sequins around the table.

Planning Table Layout

Try out where your platters will go on the table, including where you will stack the plates and how you will arrange the silverware, napkins, and any garnishes or other decorations on the table now. Remember, your goal is to move people through the line, not give them reason to dawdle, because people behind them will be waiting. Put the plates, napkins, and silverware at one side, near one another. Plan to put your pastas and salads next, followed by your main courses. If you are not serving a meal, put the cake in the center, precut, with the snacks and crudités all around it, but with the plates and napkins still to one side.

Think movement. If the room necessitates the guests enter on the left and flow right across the table, set it up that way. If you are using a round table, plan a circular flow. Physically walk around the table holding a plate. Does it feel right the way you've planned it? Move it the other way. Will fifteen women end up clumped against the wall of your dining room? Will they have to jump out the window to get back to the living room? The most common mistake is stacking plates and/or napkins at opposite ends of the buffet table. Don't do this.

Now is a fabulous time, no, it's more than that, now is the absolutely ONLY time to figure out which utensils you will use. You will destroy your careful decor if you have to put a black plastic serving spoon on your pink chiffon tablecloth. Figure now to buy or rent appropriate utensils for everything you'll be serving. Most discount gift stores sell cheap silver-plated serving utensils that will look nice for the party. If you want to dress up plain old everyday ones, tie matching ribbons to them and hot glue small silk flowers to the centers of the bows. Cut streamers short so they don't get in the food.

Garnishing Your Platters

Now's as good a time as any to think about how you will garnish these platters. You can do it with flowers, interesting toothpicks, little plastic doo-dads you bought at the party store, interesting lettuces (radicchio, romaine, Bibb), or real outside greenery, or you can make the garnishes. There are

dozens of books on garnishes, so I am going to give you directions for the two I use for wedding showers. These are so easy you'll be embarrassed by all the compliments you'll get.

Making Apple Birds

What You'll Need

Two large, unblemished red apples
Two whole cloves
Several bamboo skewers
2 T of lemon juice and a cotton ball
A paring knife
Half a potato or the second apple
Some greenery, like leaves or lettuce or parsley

How To Do It

Read these directions through before you begin cutting!

1. With a paring knife, cut just a little less than ¼ of the apple out of the whole. (Leave the remainder intact.) Don't cut all the way down to the core. This piece will become the bird's neck and head. The part directly opposite the slice-away is now the bird's body. The bottom of the apple is his little tush. Twist off the stem. This is where the head will be attached.
2. Put a little water into a bowl with the lemon juice, and put the piece you've just cut into it. Swab out the exposed section with the diluted lemon juice.

3. Leaving a gap of about ¼ inch from the exposed section, cut out the wing section by cutting a wedge from the bird's side. Don't cut all the way to the core. Repeat for other side. You will now have two thin flaps forming a V on the top of the bird.

4. Swap cuts with lemon juice, and dip the wedges into the lemon juice.

5. Take one wedge and gently slice a slightly smaller section out, creating a tiny canoe shape with even thickness. Repeat slightly smaller, then slightly smaller until only the tiniest piece of the wedge is left, barely more than the skin. You should have three or maybe four tiny apple canoes. Repeat for other side. These will become the feathers.

6. Dip them all in the lemon-juice mixture.

7. Slice the potato or other apple in half. You are now creating a stand for your bird.

8. Poke two lengths of the bamboo skewers (about 2") into the bird's body where you'd expect the legs to be. Poke the other end into the base. Check that he stands all by himself without falling over. If he does, move the skewers until he balances himself sturdily.

9. Remove the largest piece of the apple canoe or wedge from the lemon juice and put it into the crevice on the wing side of the bird, slightly off from the front. Repeat with next smallest piece and so on. Repeat on other side. If the wings keep sliding off, either blot them with a paper towel or skewer them with a toothpick. Cap the toothpick with the tiniest scrap of skin from the last cut.

10. The color contrast between the white and red makes it look like feathers. The wing will extend well behind the bird's tush.

11. For the head, take the first section you cut out of the bird. Cut a V-shape that roughly matches the depth of the V you cut in the apple by the stem when you cut this piece out. This is where you will attach the head.

12. Cut a thin neck and a head rather arrowhead shaped, coming to a point, at the opposite end. Dip in lemon juice. Attach to the neck (where the stem of the apple was) with one or two pieces of broken bamboo skewer. Trim his neck if it looks too thick.

13. Press in each whole clove to make the eyes.

14. To make a fancy tail, take the other half of an apple and cut it into a V that roughly matches the size of the V you cut out for the very first slice in step 1.

15. Repeat step 9 to make a grand feathered tail. Affix the tail with two pieces of vertical bamboo skewer. Remember to dip each slice in the lemon juice mix. Fan the pieces out and attach them with a piece or two of skewer stuck horizontally into the bird's bottom.

16. Put him where you want him—like the middle of a cheese-and-cracker platter, and garnish his base with the greenery you selected. Looks hard? It takes only about fifteen minutes the first time and has an amazing dramatic presentation.

Making Watermelon Fruit-Salad Baskets

What You'll Need

A seedless watermelon, whole, with a lovely overall color. Find one where the yellowish spot is on the bottom and when you put it on a flat surface, it doesn't roll or sit lopsided.

A sharp paring knife with a very firm blade

A large serving platter

Some sort of garnish

A melon baller

A ruler

Fruit salad ingredients

A long carving knife or electric knife

How To Do It

Read the directions completely before you begin!

1. Wash the watermelon. Put the flattest side of the watermelon down on the counter.
2. Measure the watermelon (as best you can) lengthwise. Find the center. Mark it with a pin or a tiny knick with the paring knife. Measure 1½ inches from either side. Mark where 1½ inches is. You are forming the handle of the basket.
3. With the carving knife, slice straight down on both sides from the outer markings to just about ½ inch above the horizontal middle of the watermelon.
4. Now cut from the ends <u>in</u> to the first cuts. You will now remove what is basically ¼ of the watermelon from each side of the handle. You

should have a solid watermelon half plus a wee bit more, with a three-inch wide arc over the meat.

5. Ball out all the melon inside and put in a large bowl. With the paring knife, cut the pink part off the handle, leaving just the white part exposed. Scrape out any excess with a teaspoon.

6. You now have an empty basket to hold your fruit salad. To make it pretty, however, follow the rest of the steps. Take your paring knife and cut little Vs out all the way around the edge of the lip of the basket (the horizontal cuts on the watermelon). Continue up and over the handle. Make one ½-inch slice from a right angle, and a complementary one from the right to make little Vs or triangles. Do not cut any holes in the basket part!

7. Taking your paring knife, mark a lattice pattern on the handle of the basket. Cut out the little diamond shapes all over the handle with your paring knife. Support the back of the handle (taking care not to cut yourself) when you make your slices. Or invent your own pattern.

8. Use a toothpick to attach a bow, some flowers, or anything else to the top of the handle, or tie ribbons around the sides.

9. You're done! Add other things to the balled melon, refill the basket, and voilà! An impressive fruit-salad bowl with minimum effort. However DO NOT lift the basket by its handle! Garnish the platter you will set it on anyway you desire, but flowers are particularly nice.

How to Serve Beverages

Drinks should be served at their intended temperature—coffee should be hot, melted ice cubes should not dilute iced tea, and champagne should be chilled. See the section that follows for an incredible, lovely idea for a floating ice bouquet.

It will stay solid for at least an hour and avoid diluting your drinks.

How to Make Floating Ice Bouquets

Choose two or three cheap plastic containers, like the kind Cool Whip comes in. You can also use Jell-O molds, one or more. Don't use Tupperware or some other sturdy plastic product, because you'll never get the ice bouquet out when it's frozen.

Fill each container three-quarters full with water, and float a few nontoxic flowers in it. They'll probably come to the surface. That's OK. If you want, tint the water a color that matches your party decor. Freeze solid and float in your punch bowl upside down when it's party time. They're lovely!

Remove soggy flowers and replace with backup frozen bouquets as they start to melt.

CHAPTER EIGHT

Women Bearing Gifts

Does the Hostess Traditionally Get the Bride a Gift?

It is customary for the hostess to get the bride a gift for the shower, just like everyone else. You might want to coordinate the buying of a major gift, or you might want to give her something small but very nice just from you if the shower is really setting you back financially.

We All Want to Buy Her a Big Gift. How Do I Handle That?

Does your bride need a refrigerator? A washer and dryer? A kiln for the ceramics she wants to make? Getting a big gift is exciting! You can easily keep this part of the shower a secret from the bride even if the shower isn't. If you all want to pitch in for a big gift, you might also want to read the section on wishing well showers in Chapter 2. Guests might feel empty-handed otherwise.

Here's how to get money from people—tell them you want to buy Rita and John a washer and dryer. If they know it's a big item, they're liable to put up more than the $20 they were planning on spending on a shower gift. When they hand you the money, hand them the card to sign.

What if you get through all your guests and you're still lower on cash than you can personally make up comfortably? Try calling one or two of the big donors again, or call the groom's Mom and Dad. If you get through all the guests and you have more

money than it will cost, buy relevant objects: cookware if it's a stove; a laundry basket, clothespins, detergent if it's a washer and dryer, etc.

Make sure everyone who sends money has their name on the card, even if you have to write it on yourself.

Presenting the Big Gift

You could have some handsome, burly college guys deliver it during the shower. You could have some guys set it in the front yard after she's safely inside obliviously enjoying the shower, then take her outside with all the guests to surprise her. You could have it in your living room when she gets there, with a big red bow on it. You could drape a cloth over it, stick some flowers on it, hide it in a corner of your room and ta-daa! Unveil it during the gift portion of your shower.

When Does She Open Gifts?

She can open them either before or after the food is served but probably not during. Think about the time of your shower—will the guests be ravenous when they get there? If it is potluck, will the food cool down too much while you wait?

What's the Best Way to Record What She Gets from Whom?

Make a copy of your guest list. Next to each guest's name, have a line on which you can have someone else, preferably not you, write down who gave what. Another way is to collect the cards attached to the gifts and write the object given on the back of each. Or you could simply have a sheet of paper and a pen for the guest who sits right next to the bride to list who gave what. Know this: Your bride will NOT remember and neither will you, so don't rely on her.

The Ribbon Bouquet— A Tradition of Good Luck

Assemble These Items:

- A trash can with a bag liner
- A spare paper plate
- A hole punch or sharp pencil
- Strong tape and a stapler
- Some wire twist ties
- A plastic grocery bag
- A pen and paper
- A 9"×12" manila folder
- A few cardboard boxes or crates
- The bride's car keys

There's a charming tradition to unwrapping the gifts. The bride sits in the seat of honor. Her "secretary" sits beside her (not you!). This person's job is to record who gives her what. (See "What's the Best Way to Record What She Gets from Whom?") You sit on the other side with a sturdy paper plate (preferably one that matches the shower plates) into which you have poked/punched a dozen or so holes in random order. You also have with you some strong tape or some wire twist ties and a big trash can (not a trash bag) right beside your chair.

When she unwraps each gift, she reads the card aloud, along with the name signed at the bottom. She then hands the card to the secretary and the wrappings to you. You put the wrapping paper in the trash can. (You do not use a trash bag because you'll be bending over every ten seconds, trying to open it and rearrange the paper to get it all in, and it will keep collapsing.) You take the bow and stick it through one of the holes on the plate. You either tape or wire it onto the plate firmly. Make sure you pull one through the center so she has something to hold on to. If you don't want to do this, have some other person you think is handy or crafts-oriented do this for you.

After She's Unwrapped Everything

When she's opened all the presents and you've gotten all the bows stuck to the plate, you have created the bouquet she will use at the wedding rehearsal. It's supposed to be good luck. Put the list of who gave what and all the cards into the manila folder. Now, all the wrapping paper is neatly stored in the trash can with the liner bag, so it will be easy for you to get rid of it.

Put all the gifts and the manila envelope into the crates so she can take them home, and have someone help put them in her trunk. Put the bouquet in the plastic shopping bag and put it on top so it doesn't get crushed.

What about the Gifts?
How Do I Tell Guests to Bring Them?

Most people know when they attend a shower a gift is expected—it's American female lore. So you don't need to write anything specific UNLESS it's a themed shower, in which case you need to be as specific as your theme requires. (Like: Just Lingerie, Kitchenware, Books, Things That Are Orange, you know!) It is expected and highly appropriate to tell shower guests about the location of the bridal registry. This is where the bride has hopefully listed everything she wants from a specific store, usually. That way, Brenda who is flying in for the shower from Tulsa, who hasn't seen the bride since they were fourteen, will have an idea of what sort of things her friend is into now. You should list the location and contact information for the bridal registry. Even if the guests don't buy something off the registry, it will give them an idea of her sense of taste if they take the time to investigate. And if they don't, well, that's what returns are for.

What Kinds of Gifts Are Appropriate?

The gifts that are most traditional for a wedding shower are things for the new couple's home. At themed or coed parties, the gifts are appropriate for the subject.

What If My Bride Doesn't Have a Bridal Registry?

If your bride doesn't have a registry, it could be because she's embarrassed to appear to be asking for stuff. It could be it hasn't occurred to her. It could be she didn't have time. It could be she doesn't want to.

In truth, just explain to your bride she will save three things by getting herself down to a store and setting up a bridal registry: She will save the guests at her wedding or shower from embarrassment, because they won't have to fuss and worry about getting something she will like. Lots of people have no clue how to buy a gift for someone, or how to figure out what someone else will like. Remember the worst gift someone ever gave you?

Second, she will save herself time. Yes, time. Otherwise, she's going to be doing a lot of standing in return lines after the wedding, trying to get rid of the sixteen blenders she got, or the sheets with the ghastly design sized for a queen bed when she and her groom bought a king size.

Third, she will save herself a lot of lies and embarrassment. Guests to the wedding are likely to become guests in the new couple's home in the future. And whether they admit it or not, they'll likely look around for their gift. Won't she feel silly trying to explain where she put that lovely candleholder made from glazed-on crushed potato chips, or the cuckoo clock with the little man who comes out and plays "God Save the Queen" on his harmonica.

In other words, if she doesn't have one, drive her to a store well in advance of her party and don't let her leave until she's registered.

CHAPTER NINE

Seamless
Party
Management

his section is about how to manage the people who are helping you set up the party, how to manage the guests, and how to make a backup plan in case someone falls through.

The Taming of the Shrew

First, although, of course, you always are, be polite to everyone who is helping you, whether they are being paid or not. As the tensions mount, and particularly if this is the first event you've handled, you might become a shrew. I used to become a shrew in the few hours before an event. I would just go nuts when someone called at the last minute to say they couldn't do or bring or that I had never ordered something, or something. So chill out, sister! Plan for a little bit of insanity, a touch of imperfection, and trust your own organizational skills.

Let Your Fingers Do the Talking

The second secret of good staff management is phone numbers. Yep, that's it. For everybody who says they are going to do something, write down what it is they are promising to do or bring, what their numbers are, and when they will call you to confirm that they are doing or bringing it. Call them the week before to remind them what they promised. Expect surprises. That's why you, the consummate shower thrower, have secret number three . . .

Have a Backup Plan for Your Backup Plan

While this obviously isn't brain surgery, people are the unpredictable factor in all your planning, and things will go wrong. Those of you who share my perfectionist tendencies will want to maim whoever thwarts the perfect shower you have planned, but we will avert disaster with a great backup plan.

Here's how it works:

1. If you are doing it potluck, have two of everything coming (e.g., two green salads, two casseroles, two fruit salads, etc.).

2. No matter how you are preparing the food, know that for the right price, at the last minute you can get the local deli, grocery store, or convenience package to smooth over the rough spots. No green salads? Go get the prepackaged, prewashed lettuce for $2.39 and a premade Caesar salad kit. One minute later, you've got the missing salad on the table.

3. The bakery screwed up the cake and it says "Happy Sixth Birthday, Tommy!" which you noticed after you got it home. Fine. Lose Tommy's name with a cold knife on a chilled cake. (The icing will lift right off.) Replace it with your own message, using a tube of decorator's gel (from the baking goods section). Tommy's cake is decorated like a dinosaur? Sprinkle it with some colorful flakes and a plastic whatever you bought to decorate the table with, and add some nonpoisonous flowers.

See? Everything is remedy-able. Worse things would include rain on your garden party. You would have called in advance, however, to make sure you had a backup location or a party-rental place ready to bring you a big waterproof canopy on a half-hour's notice. It might cost a bit more, but at least it won't ruin your party!

The bottom line of backup plans is: Try not to need one. Call the people you are counting on, even the professionals (bakers, caterers, musicians), to confirm a week ahead, and if you know someone is a space cadet, call also the day before. You are entitled to be nutty. In the words of the whining song from the '60s, or a very close rendition thereof: "It's my party and I'll panic if I want to, panic if I want to, panic if I want to . . . " Choose not to panic by following the steps in this book for a flawless event.

How Do I Properly Acknowledge Anyone Who Helps Me?

With the exception of a party you cohost with someone else (in which case both of your names would appear on the invitation as the hostesses), the best and easiest way to thank the people who help you is loudly and in public at the shower. Check this probable scenario out:

You are now named Martha . . .

"Oh, Martha! That's a lovely cake!" says Gertrude.

You say, "Oh yes, isn't it amazing? Pam actually baked and decorated it herself. Can you believe how great she did?" Smiling at Pam, you introduce her to Gertrude if they don't know one another.

You are now the greatest hostess in the world. See? They both think you are gracious and charming and charitable. (OK, now you can go back to your regular name.)

People love, love, love praise. People are like big dogs that like to be scratched behind the ears. Period. Even people who are shy. Really. Try it. They'll feel all warm and fuzzy inside from your kindness and your grateful acknowledgement of their contribution to your successful party. Plus, you will look totally gracious and like the perfect hostess. Oh yes, and send a sweet, short thank-you note after the shower, too. That's classy.

Countdown to the Party!

Six Weeks Before:
__ Determine your budget.
__ Select location, date, and time.
__ Decide on theme.
__ Get list of possible attendees' addresses from bride.
__ Go buy party goods or at least invitations, unless you make them by hand.

One Month Before:
__ Input names and addresses into your computer.
__ Mail invitations to your potential attendees.
__ Order the cake.
__ Select a menu.
__ Hire a caterer.

Two Weeks Before:
__ Make first RSVP calls to stragglers.
__ Start buying nonperishable food items.
__ Buy the last-minute decorations.
__ Call a local maid service.

One Week Before:
__ Confirm the cake.
__ Confirm the caterer.
__ Confirm the room.
__ Make last RSVP calls.
__ Make the party favors.
__ Call to confirm the schedule with any entertainers you have hired.

The Day Before:
__ Hang the decorations (but not paper streamers!).
__ Make the ice flower bouquets.
__ Prepare advance food.
__ Do any baking.

___ Buy any perishable grocery items.
___ Make sure you have at least three rolls of film and good flash batteries.
___ Make sure you have spare light bulbs.
___ Set up any games you will be playing.

The Morning Of:
___ Frost the cake and refrigerate it when you're done.
___ Get out every single serving utensil you will use and lay them out.
___ Set the tables, including the gift table.
___ Wash a head of romaine lettuce to garnish trays.

Two Hours Before:
___ Arrange, pick up, or have the flowers delivered.
___ Finish the decorating.
___ Finish the major cooking.
___ Put two or three stems of flowers in a bud vase in your bathroom.
___ Put a pad and pen on the chair of the person who will sit to the bride's right during gift opening.
___ Clean the litter box, spray air freshener.

One Hour Before:
___ Make sure your bathroom is sparkling clean.
___ Put an extra roll of toilet paper in an obvious but discreet place.
___ Go put on a nice outfit and do your makeup again.

Fifteen Minutes Before:
___ Add ice to the punch.
___ Put the cake on the table.
___ Light the candles.
___ Straighten up your kitchen.
___ Turn on the music—unless you hired somebody.
___ Put Kitty or Rover away so they don't get scared by guests or cause any problems.

Minding the Phone

There is one commonly known secret to all entertaining: The last few hours before the event, the phone will ring with a bunch of insanely trivial questions. It's guaranteed. If you're as sweet as apple pie, you can pick it up every time and kindly tell the callers what they need to know. Me, I don't do sweet, but you already know that from reading this book.

Now, call me evil but I never have time for all the calls before a party. And the reasons for calling always seem silly. And I'm always busy, like you'll probably be. So here are my suggestions for handling these unwelcome last minute "emergency" phone calls.

1. Get an official phone answerer—like a teenage kid. Have them answer the questions and deal with the results, and not disturb you unless it's major.
2. Put your answering machine on and screen the calls. Change your outgoing message to state, "Hi, this is Shellie. I'm getting ready for Cindy's wedding shower right now, and I cannot answer the phone. If you are calling about the shower, it's from 7:30 to 9 P.M., dress is casual, dinner will be served. The address is 213 Maple Drive, just south of Canyon View off Westcott Road. It's OK if you are going to be a little late, if you want to bring someone, or if you cannot make it at the last minute. Leave a message and let me

know what's up with you. Everybody else can leave a message, too."

Think about it: How likely is it that the stalker your Mom warned you about when you moved out on your own will be randomly dialing answering machines and get your number and address and crash the party? Not very. It's much more likely 99 percent of the calls you get during the three hours that this is your outgoing message will be from people who are related somehow to the party!

Dealing with Emergencies

Just like the Boy Scouts always say, "Be prepared!" Flat tires, people choking, someone throws up on your carpet, her ex crashes the party, your kid gets the flu that morning, aaarrrgggh! These things happen.

First of all, emotionally prepare yourself that anything can happen. The worst attitude I think you can have is "This has to be perfect." Reality check! Nobody's perfect. Most people will have a really great time and be totally oblivious to things that go wrong. It's like her wedding—and like yours. It never goes exactly as planned, and stressing out won't help.

In the case of medical emergencies, of course you'd dial 911. Brush up on the Heimlich maneuver, too, just in case. Have some local guy on call in case someone gets a flat tire or locks her keys in her car or something—not that you cannot take care of it, but it's going to take one more responsibility off your plate. Be prepared to find a replacement babysitter at the last minute for your kid(s).

Have the items in the following list on hand. You probably have most of them, but check.

Things to Have on Hand, Just in Case

A whisk broom and dustpan
An extra roll of paper towels
Bandages
Aspirin, Tylenol, Maalox
Tampons
Extra roll of toilet paper
A "Slim Jim" tool for opening locked car doors
Large trash bags
Carpet cleaner
Rubber gloves and a bucket
Safety pins
A main phone with your home phone number
   and address right nearby
Extra lightbulbs
A toilet plunger
Drain-o
A small fire extinguisher
Now you have nothing left to worry about, so stop!

Who Should Arrive First?

Depending on your situation, the bride or the guests should arrive first. If it's a surprise shower, you obviously already can answer this question.

It's wonderful if you have a bride who is willing to arrive a half hour early to help you with the last-minute stuff. She can also greet people as they come (some of whom are probably total strangers to you) and introduce people to one another. But she doesn't have to do this, of course, and probably won't want to if she's already stressed to the max from planning the wedding, or if she isn't the very social type already.

Otherwise, your guests should be scheduled to arrive half an hour before the bride. This way, latecomers still are there in time when the bride walks in and when the bride gets there, she sees a huge pile of presents neatly arranged on the table you've decorated, waiting for her. She also walks into a room full of friends, which is a very nice feeling.

I'll Never Forget Ol' What's-Her-Name!

OK, so assuming all your guests don't know each other, the nicest thing any hostess can do is provide name tags. Sounds silly for fifteen women in a small apartment for two hours? Nope. There's nothing worse than Elizabeth having a twenty-minute conversation on your sofa with Janet, and then at the end, neither one remembers the other's name.

Get a package of name tags from the stationery department at the drugstore or stationery store. Get a huge magic marker (preferably in a matching color) and write everyone's name on it. If you want to be artsy, use glitter glue. Have them waiting by the door so that as people come in and you or the bride greets them, you can stick it onto their dresses—and be wearing one yourself. Since everyone will know your bride, make hers elaborate with bits of lace and ribbons, if you like, and simply say "Bride" on it.

What Do We Do During the Shower?

The main events of a shower are eating and unwrapping gifts. You can add party games or some other activity if you want, and you can add dancing for a coed shower. If it's a surprise party, the other main event is seeing the bride's surprise when she walks in.

Do We Eat Before or After the Gifts Are Opened?

Ah, here you get to use your discretion! If you've got lots of people and thus zillions of presents to open, and you've scheduled this near a mealtime, you'll have hungry, bored guests watching the bride open the mountain of presents. But if you feed them before, people will be juggling cake plates on their laps while they are trying to ooh and aah and maybe even pass for inspection the lovely gifts you all bring her.

At my own wedding shower, we ate first. At my first baby shower, we ate cake after the gifts were opened, and one guest was horrified at this departure from what she perceived as custom.

Figure it this way. If you're personally going to be stressed out that something will be too hot or cold if you open gifts first, because you are catering it yourself or doing it potluck, then eat first. If you think it's going to be a bother to have plates and glasses all over your house when people are hanging around watching her open gifts, then eat later. Especially if you're worried about spills. Or you could serve hors d'oeuvres before and the meal after. Make this part easy on yourself, and damn the etiquette torpedoes.

Does the Bride Have Any Responsibilities During the Shower?

In a perfect world, your friend would have figured this out all alone, but if the world isn't perfect where you live, you can tell her that you'd love her to come half an hour early to help you greet people. She should also be willing to introduce people to one another, especially from different spheres of her life. Other than that, she's there just to have fun. Ask her what she wants to do, if anything.

What Is the Order in Which Things "Should" Happen?

The first answer to this question is, However you want! The second, traditional, answer is this:

1. People arrive.
2. Bride arrives.
3. People chat and nibble.
4. Eat food.
5. Gifts opened.
6. Game or two played.
7. Party favors doled out.
8. People leave.
9. You crash.

CHAPTER TEN

Cha-Cha-Cha Choices:

Getting the Music Right

M usic is such a personal thing! Some people are heavily influenced by the sounds around them, and for them, playing sad or melancholy at your party would be a real downer. Further, some folks don't like rock and roll (hard to imagine, isn't it?), and some very intense people might be offended by Led Zeppelin lyrics. Unless you've chosen a shower that has a musical theme, for example, Elvis Commemorative or Nifty '50s, you're going to have to think a bit about what you want to play.

First, do you and your bride want the music to be mellow and refined? Classical would be nice, but it's often interruptive at a party to have cymbals clashing. If you are going classical, which is an excellent choice for most parties, may I suggest you pick up a Baroque medley CD? Did you know that Baroque music actually stimulates the cerebral cortex of the brain and generates fresh ideas? (This was allegedly tested on a number of employees in big corporations.)

If serenity is the key to your party—try Enya's *Shepherd Moon*, a Gregorian Chant, Vivaldi's *Four Seasons*, Celine Dion's *C'est Deux*, anything from Wyndham Hill, Narada, Wynton Marsalis, or James Galway. Looking for something more rowdy? Pick your favorites and ask the bride hers. Or try the tried-and-true party favorites for thirty-somethings—Rod Stewart, Billy Joel, Bruce Springsteen, The Eagles, and so on.

Right now there are a lot of "golden oldies" and "dance classics" CDs around you can pick up for under $10 usually. I'm not happy to admit that some of my favorite songs are now available in montage. (I once read that the definition of growing older is "Your favorite music is now available through television ads for two easy payments on your credit card"—It's a scary thing!)

You should have, borrow, or rent a nice stereo system for the party. Set the speakers in opposite corners in the main room for the party, and test them in advance.

CHAPTER ELEVEN

Great Shower Activities,

or How to Entertain a Bunch of Women for two Hours

Being a hostess can be fun. In the words of my dear friend Amy, the goal of any party is for the hostess to walk in and have fun, and the details to take care of themselves. This is going to happen only with careful planning, which is something you have done as you worked through this book.

As hostess, you not only want to have fun, you want to make sure your bride has lots and lots of fun, and your guests do, too. You want it to be enjoyable, comfortable, and memorable. This is easy. You just have to work from the opposite perspective: The deal is, you have to make sure you don't make anyone feel uncomfortable.

Following Your Theme

If you've chosen a theme from this book, chances are there's a shower game that's perfect for it, and it was mentioned in the theme description. There may be other games that would be perfect for the type of girls you and your bride are.

Doing a Funny Skit

If anyone in your set can write, sing, dance, or act, or if anyone should have been a comedian and missed her calling, why not put together these talented folks and create a special ten- or fifteen-minute skit for the shower? Steal ideas from Letterman, Leno, or Raphael, or make up something totally on your own.

Memories Activity

Have everyone bring a photo of the bride or groom or themselves with her. Assemble them into a montage. Write on the back where each one was taken and the memory associated with it. Or collect written memories and put them in a memory book for the bride, with or without the pictures.

Getting to Know You

Working in a circle, have everyone tell how they first met the bride, or tell a funny story about their experiences with her.

Not Him Again!

Is your bride so annoyingly besotted by her beloved she's driving everyone nuts? Try this game every time she mentions his name or anyone says a different word, like "work" or "cat." Choose a word that no one is allowed to say at the party. Before the party, select a bunch of really cheesy segments from movies, erotica books, or paperback romances. As in: "Her perky breasts heaved at the sight of him. Oh, when would she feel the weight of his tawny fingers on her smooth young skin? Cybil noted that her nipples were hardening under her shirt. Would Jim notice? Would he care?" (You could also make them up, like I just did.)

Anytime someone mentions the groom's name, or some other forbidden word, he or she has to pull one of these selections. Type them on sheets of paper and put them into a big bag or box. The guest has to read it aloud, with inflection. Hysterical!

This Is Your Life!

Having a "This Is Your Life!" shower would be loads of fun if your guests include family and friends who may not know each other. Get each of your guests who RSVPs to tell you their favorite anecdote about the bride. Ask for pictures. Call her mom and get background information such as when she was born, the type of labor mom had, and so forth.

If you've got dramatic flair, tape-record a baby crying as your intro, with "It's a girl!" as a voice-over. Continue with a "Jennifer Sexton—(drum roll)—This is your life!" Then, emcee a wonderful journey through the bride's life. To make it even more fun, try to invite her best friend from out of town (high school) whom she hasn't talked to in years, or the bride's sister from Georgia who told her she couldn't make it, or anyone else you think your bride would go nuts to see. If you cannot get a relative or an old friend, why not hire her favorite author (Authors eat up this type of chance to be a big star! You'll have to pay airfare, though, and a night's lodging.) Try getting her favorite English teacher from grammar school, someone like that. Do some investigating to find out whom she'd most love to see. Put them up at your house if you have to.

If you are going to do this, play it not more than thirty minutes into the shower, so the surprise guest gets to enjoy the party, too, and not just wait in the wings, and so that the late guests (there are always a few) won't miss the fun.

Entertaining Ideas

Talent you might hire for your shower could include:

1. Harpist
2. Violinist
3. Clown
4. Magician
5. Belly dancer
6. Masseuse
7. Manicurist
8. Dancer
9. Stripper
10. Pianist
11. Mime
12. Actor
13. Author
14. Psychic
15. Astrologer
16. Palm reader
17. Comedian
18. Artist

Hire a Local Marriage, Love, Sex, or Relationship Book Author

I'm partial to this idea for a number of reasons. To find a local author, call your biggest local bookstore and ask if they know someone. Call the local branch of PEN if you are in a big city, or look under "Publisher's Representatives" or "Literary Agents" in the Yellow Pages. These people probably know someone. Short of that, call the local library. There's bound to be someone. Get this person in to read a bit from their book, offer them some cake. If you want them to do it for free, tell them you'll put the book on display and/or let them sell copies afterward. Authors are natural-born hams for the most part, especially those who write on these topics. And the best part? You get an amusing diversion for free!

Hiring a Palm Reader, Astrologer, or Psychic

What an incredibly trendy and fun twist to your shower! If you don't know anyone who does this kind of thing, ask around! One of your friends is bound to be able to give you a recommendation. After you get the recommendation, go visit this person yourself! Yep, get a reading. See what you think about them. Then ask them if they would be willing to do the shower. Chances are strong the answer will be yes, as most of these professionals don't make a lot of money. Write up a short contract that says, "Zelda the Magnificent will attend a wedding shower at (location) on (date, time) and perform readings for all who wish it, not to exceed (number of) people. In deference to this contract,

I make a deposit of $75 (I wouldn't put down more than that!) toward this event, the balance of $(agreed-on remainder) to be paid at the completion of the party."

Have her and you sign it. Don't take chances. My experience with the majority of these professionals is they spend a lot of time living in other universes and aren't always great about contracts and things. Call a few days before and also the day of the shower to be sure.

Make sure you set up a private room for Zelda to do the readings in, and have your guests pencil in the time of their reading.

Hiring an Impersonator

From Mae West to Abe Lincoln to Barbara Walters to the president, good and bad impersonators are everywhere. Think of all the *Saturday Night Live* skits you've seen! An impersonator may be just the right touch for your event. To hire one, call a local speakers' bureau, or you can find any impersonator you want by calling ForthWrite Speakers Bureau (my agent's company) in Malibu, California, at 310-457-5785. The impersonator can show up in person, or just do it over the phone.

How to Hire a Male Dancer/Stripper

While this may be the domain of the bachelorette party, you might choose to do it at the shower, assuming you won't freak out any of the guests. How do you find the right guy? First, look in the Yellow Pages under "Dancers." (Some Classifieds sections will offer this, too.) Call no less than six places—the ones with the half-page Yellow Pages ads will be more expensive than the one with the fine print that says, "Joe's Male Strippers and TV Repair Shop." Make a selection.

If the person who answers the phone is a jerk, or rude, find another place to call. Get prices from six people. Tell them your party date, what the event is, and ask what they provide. (Own music? More than ten minutes of dancing? Any interaction with the guest of honor?)

Narrow it down to two or three, and go see the guys who will actually be stripping/dancing. From there, you can probably make a good choice all by yourself. Remember to confirm his engagement a few days before the party.

How to Hire Any Talent

Hiring someone to entertain your bride and your guests at the party is always fun, although it may be a bit pricey. If you don't know anyone who will give you a cut-rate or who would do it for free because they are a friend, you'll have to hire someone.

First, figure out what would work best for your location and the type of guests you are having and when you are having the shower. Then, look in the Yellow Pages under the appropriate word. (Some newspapers' Classifieds sections might offer help, too.) Call no less than six places—the ones with the half-page Yellow Pages ads will be more expensive than the one with the fine print that says, "Margie's Trained Animal Act and Hair Salon." Make a selection.

If the person who answers the phone is a jerk, or rude, find another place to call. Get prices from six people. Tell them your party date, what the event is, and ask what they provide for your money. Ask them to send you a brochure and a referral list. I might hire someone who didn't have a brochure (probably because they'd be cheaper), but I would NEVER hire someone who couldn't provide me with a list of satisfied customers!

Narrow it down to two or three, and go see the per-former live. Ask them if you can crash their next gig for ten minutes, or if you can have a demo tape, or whatever. Somehow, make sure they can do what they are promising and that you aren't the first person who is buying from them. Not much is worse than a really bad entertainer. Your guests will be trapped!

From there, you can probably make a good choice all by yourself. It's customary to put 50 percent down to hold the date. Remember to confirm the engagement a few days before the party. If they don't show, have a backup of one of the games in this book—and get your money back.

Take Them Dancing

It wouldn't be totally out of place to organize your wedding shower around something interesting, like a group dancing lesson. You could drag everyone down to the local Arthur Murray studio (after the cake and presents) and let them all learn how to cha-cha. Make sure your bride will be playing cha-cha music at the reception!

Otherwise, you could take them all to a water park, a nightclub, a miniature-golf course, or any other diversion that your bride would love and the guests might enjoy, too. Some of these places might have a room for special events like yours—you could hold the whole thing right there!

Get a Piñata!

A piñata is a hollow papier-mâché object, often made to look like a person or animal. You can get them at the party store, or if you live in a neighborhood with a Hispanic section, you can buy a better one there for probably 1/3 what you'd pay at the party store.

The deal with piñatas, which are de rigueur at kid's parties, is that they are fun. The adults wistfully watch kids at kids' parties, so why not make one for your adults' party?

The piñata is filled with wrapped candy and/or little surprises. You need not fill the whole thing, just at least half. The opening is sealed (usually with Elmer's glue!) and the piñata is hung at the end of a long rope. The rope is then slung over a tree, creating a sort of pulley with the piñata on one end. When the rope is pulled, the piñata slides up and down in space and wiggles around. You will want to have someone managing the rope-pulling during this game.

When the guests are ready, you line them up shortest to tallest. You blindfold the first one and give her a base-ball bat. She's supposed to hit the moving piñata and burst it open, spilling the contents. She gets three swings. If she doesn't crack open the swaying piñata, the bat and blind-fold go to the next woman. And so on.

Don't play this game if you have men at your shower—they get way too competitive and nutty. But women might think it's fun. When the thing is finally hit hard enough to crack open, the candy/small gift items/tiny perfume sam-ples, whatever you filled it with, spill out and the idea is everyone is supposed to scramble for the contents.

Getting grown women to scramble for the contents might be a little hard, so before the game, announce you've put a special copper penny into one candy wrapper and whoever finds it wins . . . a prize? An all-expense-paid lunch for two with the bride? Your choice!

Let the Games Begin

Games can be loads of fun at parties! They break the ice, heat up the conversation, and get guests actively involved. There are games obviously related to the party theme, and then there are traditional shower games.

Some games include:

Pin the Boutonniere on the Groom: In this game you use a big picture of the groom (instead of a donkey). Don't think too long about the double entendre of that one! Using a blown-up photo of the groom, blindfold the guests, and they try to pin a paper or silk flower onto his left lapel.

Wedding Trivial Pursuit: The bride supplies you with trivia about her dating experience. Use a Trivial Pursuit board you have modified and question cards made by you from index cards.

Bridal Bloopers: Someone writes down the bride's words as she opens her gifts at the shower. "Oh, it's so pretty!" "I've always wanted one of these!" and so on. Then someone reads them back in a list under the heading: "What Jennifer will say on her wedding night." This traditional party game is hilarious!

Wedding Shower Jeopardy: The hostess puts together a bunch of trivia answers about the bride and groom. Then ask the guests to phrase the questions. Things like, *Answer:* "The waiter spilled water on the table." *Question:* "What happened on Brittany and Jeff's first date?"

Shower Charades: Collect a bunch of wedding and marriage axioms or quotes or old traditions (like "something old, something new . . ."). Write them on bits of paper. Guests choose them from a white high-heeled shoe or a bridesmaid's hat or something like that. Separated into two teams, one player acts out the phrase for their team members so they can guess the phrase.

Bridal Herstory: You write out a humorous story, in advance of the shower, preferably on one of those large newsprint flip charts. (They cost about $2 at the arts and crafts store.) You leave blanks for some of the nouns, verbs, and adjectives. At the party, you fill in the story with the words guests call out to you to create a funny story about the bride and groom.

Lucky Girl: On the bottom of the paper cups in which beverages will be served, write the bride's name, groom's name, and other wedding-related words (veil, gown, bouquet, etc.). Put all the words on matching slips of paper. The bride picks one slip of paper out of a hat or jar during the party. Whoever has that particular word on the bottom of her cup wins a small prize.

Conducting a Raffle

A raffle or two can be lots of fun at a shower. Pick out one or two funny, cute, or pretty prizes, usually not exceeding $20 each in cost. You can also collect some trivial prizes—plastic blow horns and funny party hats. Make some sort of a system whereby guests can win. Like, the guest whose slice of cake has a thimble in it (and who doesn't choke on it!) gets a prize. Or write numbers on the bottom of the cups, and have the bride draw a number from a hat. The guest with that number on her cup wins a prize.

Or, make it be based on something besides luck. Who knows the bride's grandma's native country? Who knows the groom's middle name? Or give prizes to the winners of the games we've just talked about.

Getting Prizes Donated to Your Shower

This might take a bit of pluck, but you certainly have that by now! To get prizes donated, decide what you want. A buy-one-get-one-free dinner from a local restaurant? A free soda with a to-go lunch order from the deli on the corner? A free dozen donuts? Ten dollars off from the lingerie store? All you gotta do is call a couple of small, independent retailers in your area and you'll have prizes coming out of your ears!

Pitch it like this, in person, to the manager or owner:

"Hi, my name is Gloria. I'm hosting a party for one of my friends who is getting married. We'll be having about twenty local women. I've always loved your corned-beef-and-peanut-butter-on-rye sandwiches here, so I was thinking, 'Wouldn't it be fun if you offered a free one to someone who wins one of the party games?' You'd come to the attention of all twenty women, and maybe expand a little business. Who knows? Whoever wins the CB&PB on rye might get as addicted as I am and become a regular. Whaddya say?"

They'll either say Yes!, Well, how about a free Coke if they buy the sandwich instead, or No, honey, but here's a french fry for your troubles. It's easy! When s/he says yes, pull out the preprinted gift certificate (their store's name nicely preprinted with the address) and write on the blank line what they are providing. Have them sign it and give it an expiration date (six months is perfect). Great! Now you have a valuable prize that didn't cost you more than a few pennies!

Or, think of which attendees have their own businesses and get them to donate something. Retail stores especially love this kind of opportunity.

Let Them Eat Cake!

In summary of all these activities, themes, games, party ideas, raffles, and what not, it really is about your girlfriend who's getting married. It's about celebrating and supporting her choice, and making her feel like she has a team of loving friends supporting her and sharing in her bliss.

If you want to, just put on some nice music, gather a group of friends, and let them eat cake!

CHAPTER TWELVE

Parting Gifts

Taking Great Pictures of the Shower

Little is more fun than a Polaroid at a party. Catch your guests being funny or sweet and create momentoes they will always cherish. Call local camera shops to see if you can rent a Polaroid. (Polaroid cameras produce the pictures right away. They're more expensive and the emulsion deteriorates more quickly, but they are fun in the moment.)

Do Yourself a Favor!
Create Memories to Go

If you are the least bit crafts-oriented, this will probably be your favorite part of the preparations. The best part is, you can do the favors tomorrow—they keep! That way, you'll be all set. First, how many do you make? I suggest you make five more than you think you'll need. What's the worst that can happen? You have some left over. I've left at least one idea with each party theme for you to choose from.

Now, I've heard it said, "Grown women do not get or give party favors." Wrong! You want your guests to have a totally memorable time? Party favors say, "Thanks for participating" and give a pile of warm fuzzy feelings the next morning when she wakes up and sees it where she left it when she got home the night before!

So how do you do it? Well, I'm going to give you the easy way, because heck, some of you will get way more creative, and some of you will think even what I've suggested here is slave labor. Here are my easy steps to creating party favors.

First, answer this question Yes or No:

I am armed with a glue gun and I know how to use one (without third-degree burns).

If you answered Yes, you'll do great. If you answered No, you will learn with this project. Otherwise, try to get someone who's into this kind of thing to do this.

For the purpose of convenience, I am going to assume you have fifteen people coming to the shower, and you will therefore prepare twenty party favors.

Go to a crafts store. Look under "Party Supplies" in your Yellow Pages. They will have these adorable precut veil circles, about 6 inches in diameter, with ruffled (fluted) edges. Buy a package.

Go to where they sell little plastic wedding stuff. Like champagne glasses, little slippers, pretend rings, stuff like that. They'll have a display of ideas right there for you to choose from. Steal their ideas, that's a good thing, or just do what I'm about to tell you. Buy twenty pieces of some sort of plastic thing—let's say the champagne glasses. Buy a few sprays of wired beaded pearl sprays and some curling ribbon in the color(s) of her wedding/your shower.

Buy a glue gun and a package of glue sticks if you don't have them already. (Better, cheaper, longer-lasting serious glue guns are at the hardware store, but the silly pink ones at the crafts store will work just fine unless you plan to put in some serious hours with it in the future.) Buy ¼ cup per guest of some kind of candy, like Jordan almonds, or ½ cup per guest of some sort of potpourri.

OK, get out your glue gun, pinking shears, scissors, and a bowl. Dump the filling stuff (potpourri or candy) into the bowl. You're ready to go. Slap one piece of precut veil onto the middle of your clean work surface. Take ½ cup of potpourri or a handful of candy into the middle. Gather it up into a sachet/package or bundle. If you are really worried about sealing it, use a small rubber band now, but it's not really necessary. (*Hint:* To make the potpourri sachets look plumper, put a cluster of five cotton balls or a tiny Styrofoam ball in the center before you seal the sachet!)

If you want your favor to hang, like a Christmas ornament, then take an 8-inch-long piece of ribbon and tie it tightly into a knot at one end. Hold it sideways, against the side of the sachet (see Illust.), and pull one end lengthwise through the other end. To secure the entire package, wrap another length of ribbon around it and double wrap it. Gather it up into a package and tie it tightly with a piece of ribbon. Tie it into a bow. Double knot the bow.

Now, take your plastic doo-dad and a pearl spray. With your hot glue gun, melt a drop of glue onto the very center of the bow. Count to five so the glue cools enough not to melt the cheap plastic doo-dad. Press in the pearl spray. Then press the plastic doo-dad firmly into the warm glue. Or, you could tie the doo-dad onto the ends/ streamers of the ribbon. This will have to be your choice when you are assembling the projects. Voila! There you have it! That was easy, wasn't it? Stick all the favors in a long low box and you're done!

What You Need to Make Twenty Potpourri or Candy Sachets as Shower Favors

- ✿ 20 precut 6-inch veil/net circles
- ✿ 20 little wedding trinkets (champagne glasses, slippers, wedding rings, etc.)
- ✿ A roll of curling ribbon in matching wedding colors OR 10 yards of $\frac{1}{3}$ inch satin ribbon
- ✿ Enough sprays of beaded pearls to make 20 pieces (they often come 6 per unit)
- ✿ $\frac{1}{4}$ cup of some kind of candy, per sachet, OR $\frac{1}{2}$ cup of prescented potpourri, per sachet
- ✿ 5 cotton balls (if you are doing the potpourri)
- ✿ A hot glue gun
- ✿ Scissors or pinking sheers
- ✿ A bowl for putting the filling in
- ✿ A measuring cup (optional)
- ✿ 20 small rubber bands (optional)
- ✿ A long low box for putting the completed projects in

Other Ideas for Party Favors

Some favors are completely indicated by the type of party you are having! Consider these ideas, which are copied from Chapter 2. Something here might spark an idea, even if it was originally intended for a party with a different theme than yours!

1. Plastic leis to wear
2. Packages of food tied in Hawaiian fabric
3. Fake sunglasses

4. Boxed petit fours
5. Filled, sealed plastic champagne glasses
6. A red panty "rose"
7. Condom wrapped in lace
8. A garter belt
9. A small decorated straw hat
10. Something—small cornbreads? chili mix?— tied up in kerchiefs
11. Little bottles of tanning lotion
12. Sunglasses
13. Bath tea sachets
14. Little pots or baskets filled with tea bags
15. Anything Fourth of July, New Year's, or other major holiday
16. A flower or topiary in a pot
17. A cut flower tied with a ribbon
18. A seed packet
19. A tiny trowel with a bow
20. Wooden spoons tied with ribbons or with the bride's name painted on them
21. Spice holders made from yarn and cinnamon sticks
22. Keychains with tiny hammers or screwdrivers
23. A few sheets of writing paper and envelopes, wrapped nicely
24. Cupcakes decorated with monopoly houses
25. Little containers or bags filled with bath beads
26. A discount coupon for a haircut or manicure
27. Little alcohol bottles tied with ribbon
28. Spools of white thread with a note tied with ribbon through the center that says
     "Thank you for coming"
29. Coupons/tickets to a postwedding party you plan to hold
30. Gift certificates to Blockbuster
31. Bottles of CD cleaner with ribbons around their necks

32. Those big dopey gauze hair bonnets our moms wore—or plastic rainbonnets
33. Lace handkerchiefs
34. Big floppy sun hats you decorated in advance and everyone wore at the party
35. The project guests made at whatever art workshop you took them to (ceramics, stained glass, etc.)
36. A map of the state or city, with directions to the wedding drawn on it
37. Lots of bubble gum
38. A pair of bobby socks
39. Little satin pillows
40. Sleep masks
41. A three-prong adapter you painted with fabric paint
42. An extension cord
43. A wreath of laurel leaves (silk or real)
44. A brightly colored "Egyptian" armband made from electrician's wire
45. Something else in keeping with the theme of the costumes for the shower—like quill pens if you did a patriotic shower
46. A copy of a book that was featured or read from
47. Admission to any class you provided, like a dance class of some type
48. A brightly colored cardboard flower or peace sign
49. A red gingham checked cloth napkin or two
50. Boxed chocolates
51. A tiny satin lingerie or jewelry case
52. A quilted square
53. A sampler of cheeses
54. A bottle of wine
55. A wine glass with the guest's name on it
56. A shower cap
57. A set of chopsticks
58. A silk lipstick case

CHAPTER THIRTEEN

Cleanup Tricks

*Y*ou were a perfect hostess. The party was flawless and your bride had a lovely time. There was enough good food for everyone, everyone seems to have had fun, she enjoyed herself thoroughly, and, truth be told, so did you.

You used paper plates and napkins; you remembered to put the leftovers into the fridge before you crashed last night. Now you crawl out of bed, slip into jeans, and wander into the kitchen (which is a disaster) for a cup of coffee. You sit down for half an hour, glancing calmly at the wreckage that is your home. You stretch your legs out, read a magazine, and wait. What are you waiting for? The doorbell to ring, of course! And when it does, you open the door to the one or two maids you hired from the local maid service. They will have your place back to spotless in two hours, while you finish your magazine and take "Thank-you-I-had-a-great-time" calls from your bride and the guests.

Ah, life is perfect. You send a quiet good wish to this writer, saying, "Gee, Jennifer. You were right! It's much more important to have the house spotless after the party than it was the day of the party!" You muse how the simple truth I shared—that after five people get to your house, no one notices how dirty or clean it is—is a universal hosting truth.

When the maids leave at last, your house all tidy and fresh smelling, and you give them the check, you thank your lucky stars that you bought this book. Then you trot off to the mall.

Index

H

I

J

EVERYTHING

The Everything Wedding Book, 2nd Edition
*by Janet Anastasio, Michelle Bevilacqua,
and Stephanie Peters*

This completely revised edition is packed with information, checklists, calendars, budgeting ideas, and advice and insights on:

* Handling the stickiest situations
* Ceremony and reception ideas the bride and groom can use that will make everyone happy without losing their cool or their shirt
* The steps to follow to find the right attire, caterer, reception site, flowers, musician, photographer, and anything else they need.

Trade paperback, 384 pages
1-58062-190-2, $12.95

* Advice on how to make it through alive when dealing with scheduling, budgeting, and other nitty-gritty tasks
* And everything else anyone needs to know to plan the perfect wedding!